Beneath The Surface:

Unearthing The Seedbed
Of Anxiety And Depression

Marjorie A. Smith

"When solving problems, dig at the roots instead of just hacking at the leaves."

— Anthony J. D'Angelo

I dedicate *Beneath the Surface: Unearthing the Seedbed of Anxiety and Depression* to my amazingly wonderful husband, Darryl Smith. Darryl, sweetheart, I am eternally thankful for you and your unconditional love and support. You are the epitome of the word *love*. You've seen me at my worst and loved me anyway. Thank you for standing in faith with and for me when I couldn't stand for myself. Thank you for caring for me when I couldn't care for myself. Thank you for covering me with consistency, patience, and grace. Thank you for being my safe place. You truly embrace and exemplify the commitment of the vows we shared so many years ago. My life is richer because of you! I will love you forever!

A great big thank you to my children: Brandon, Kristian, and Latrice. You guys will never know how much your love and support empowered me and helped me fight the good fight of faith. For fear of leaving anyone out, I also thank those who listened, let me cry, and lifted me up. You know who you are, and I am forever thankful. I love you all. I also want to thank those who were well-meaning. This book will help you understand that the struggle is real and help you learn how you can support those who simply need love and grace.

I would like to thank the following medical practitioners who were a part of my healing journey: Dr. Eudene Harry, Dr. Marissa Magsino, Dr. Lesli Leimer, Pam Wesley, Lisa Beaury, Dr. James Dail, Dr. J. Mendez, and Dr. Sharon Thetford. The Bible teaches that there is safety in a multitude of counselors, and I wholeheartedly agree. Each of them understood and helped me understand that a holistic approach to wellness is essential for health and wholeness.

CONTENTS

DISCLAIMER: The information provided in this book is designed to provide helpful information on the subjects discussed. Its contents are the experiences, expressions, and opinions of its author. This book is not meant to be used, nor should it be used, to diagnose, treat, cure, or prevent any medical condition or disease. For diagnosis or treatment of any medical problem, always consult your healthcare professional.

FOREWARD

Wow, what an amazing ride! When the Lord joined Marjorie and me together in holy matrimony thirty-seven years ago, we had no real clue about the roller-coaster ride—the journey—life would take us on over the years ahead. At the time, all we had was our love for each other and the Lord's love for us, both of which helped us reach the point in life where are today. We have not reached our final destination, and I feel like we are only halfway there after all these years together.

Before pioneering and planting a church and starting our pastoral ministries together, my twenty-five-year career as an officer in the U.S. Air Force offered us many journeys, opportunities, and challenges. However, we never faced anything as challenging as Marjorie's battle with anxiety and depression, which began approximately two years after my military retirement. You have to read her story for yourself! As I read it, it evokes wide-ranging emotions for me—from tears of sorrow as I recall some horrible moments on our journey to tears of joy as I reflect on Marjorie's freedom from the emotional and physical bondages caused by anxiety and depression. As stated by the lyrics of the famous Christian hymn "Amazing Grace" (Newton 1779):

> *Through many dangers, toils, and snares*
> *I have already come;*
> *'Tis Grace hath brought me safe thus far*
> *And Grace will lead me home.*

I thank the Lord for Marjorie, and I thank Him for His Grace! He has given Marjorie such an amazing story to tell. I highly recommend this book to everyone dealing with anxiety and depression and everyone who may know someone dealing with it—that practically includes almost everyone. Marjorie's unique combination of candor, care, concern, and compassion resonates throughout this book and will make a huge difference in the life of every person who reads it. She always said she would share her story—so here it is—in a powerful and life-changing way!

— G. Darryl Smith

INTRODUCTION

I UNDERSTAND

"Those who judge will never understand, and

those who understand will never judge."

-Wilson Kanadi

Everyone yearns to be understood. How often have you heard someone say, "you don't understand?" How many times have you uttered these words? How did it make you feel when you were misunderstood? Isn't it frustrating and aggravating when someone doesn't understand what you are saying, feeling, or going through? Isn't it even more disappointing when someone won't even make an effort to try and understand? Of course, it is.

Maybe I haven't experienced exactly what you are experiencing, but I can empathize with you because I choose to honor you as a human. I can love you, genuinely listen, and offer whatever support and care that I can. It's quite simple as Ephesian 4:2 states, "Be humble and gentle in every way. Be patient with each other and lovingly accept each other" (GW).

Galatians 6:2 teaches us to share each other's burdens, and in this way, you will obey the law of Christ (NLT).

I've learned that anxiety and depression are already cruel and relentless in their judgment of you, so the last thing you need is the judgment of those who don't understand and those who don't care to understand. Trust me…I UNDERSTAND.

I UNDERSTAND what it's like living with paralyzing anxiety and depression.

I UNDERSTAND the long tormenting nights of insomnia, wanting so desperately to sleep.

I UNDERSTAND what it's like to look at the telephone and feel too overwhelmed to answer.

I UNDERSTAND the uncontrollable crying episodes and feeling condemned because I was crying so much.

I UNDERSTAND what it's like to feel so bad, so weak, that I was unable to get out of bed.

I UNDERSTAND the horror of waking up in a full panic attack.

I UNDERSTAND the mental and physical exhaustion of repeated panic attacks.

I UNDERSTAND the zombie-like state caused by taking prescription anti-anxiety medications.

I UNDERSTAND feeling like a guinea pig as doctors "tried" different medications that didn't work.

I UNDERSTAND what it's like taking depression medication(s) that made me psychotic.

I UNDERSTAND the guilt, shame, and self-condemnation.

I UNDERSTAND trying to "act normal" as anxiety thunders throughout my body.

I UNDERSTAND the conflict of trying to pray for and encourage others when struggling to pray for and encourage myself.

I UNDERSTAND what it's like to routinely stand in the pulpit, preach, go home, and crawl back in bed.

I UNDERSTAND the tormenting thought: when will I ever get better?

I UNDERSTAND how it feels thinking I was a burden to my family.

I UNDERSTAND what it's like to battle feelings of hopelessness…feeling like a failure.

I UNDERSTAND the defeating thoughts: Why can't I shake this? What is wrong with me?

I UNDERSTAND the humiliation of finally sharing and asking for help only to be told, "you just need to pray and trust God."

I UNDERSTAND questioning my faith and my ability to trust God.

I UNDERSTAND what it's like to go to bed thinking, "If I don't wake up, it will be just fine with me".

I UNDERSTAND what it's like to fight unrelenting thoughts of suicide and death.

I UNDERSTAND how it feels to begin weaning off anxiety medication and being afraid of the potential for increased anxiety and/or other unpleasant side effects.

I UNDERSTAND how it feels to be angry: angry with myself and angry with others.

I UNDERSTAND the daily struggle, the relentless stress of hiding, the isolation, the persistent and strong lies of the enemy, the stigma, the fear of being found out, and the overwhelming sense of shame while fighting anxiety and depression. Looking back, I now know that the weight of all this contributed to and made my journey harder than it needed to be.

So my dear friend, I truly do understand. I know full well the angst—and now I *know* and *understand* the triumph and victory that is possible.

Let me tell you…You, too, can know this freedom. I have been where you are. I know what you are going through. I have experienced what you are experiencing, and I am here to tell you that you're not alone. You're simply in a difficult season of life right now. I want you to know that just like the weather, storms never last forever. The sun will shine again.

I want you to know that even though my life was a living hell for three long years, I was able to unearth the seedbed (the root causes) of anxiety and depression in my life and gain victory over them. Seeds produce roots and there is always a root to every problem we face. We just have to look beneath the surface to get to the root(s).

Now, let me be honest with you. I don't want to mislead you in any way. My journey was not easy, and it was not overnight. It was a process, and it was absolutely and positively a God thing. I give all glory and honor to God because He provided the way of escape for me (1 Cor. 10:12–13, E S V).

I want to share with you what I learned during this ordeal and let you know that you, too, can triumph over anxiety and depression. God doesn't love me anymore than He loves you. What God did for me, He can do for you.

I was that girl suffering from anxiety and depression, but I refused to let it define me. Instead, God is now using what I've been through to help define the path I am taking toward my destiny. Part of my destiny is helping you unearth anxiety and depression in your life.

It's not too late for you to get your life back. You have been destined for so much more. God created you for a purpose on this earth. You have gifts, talents, and abilities that this world needs. Do not allow anxiety and depression to steal your shine. It's your time, my friend. Are you ready to begin walking toward your destiny?

No man-made diagnosis has the power to determine, destroy, or derail your destiny. Instead, decide to allow every pain, every tear, and every struggle serve as fuel to propel you into your purpose.

CHAPTER 1 - I AM

"I am unique. I am special. I am me."

-Unknown

Hi there. I am Marjorie. I was never particularly fond of my name. I've only met one person my age with my name. A few years ago, I discovered that Marjorie means child of light, a pearl, and a jewel. A pearl is beautiful, unique, and rare. It is created by God and requires no cutting or polishing by man. Well, that's me. I am God's creation, and He is the one who does all the work in and through my life.

I am a wife, mother, and grandmother as well as a daughter, sister, cousin, sister-in-law, auntie, friend, and mentor. My family is everything and I enjoy spending quality time with them. I love spending time at the beach watching the waves crash against the shore; it's my happy place. I enjoy long nature walks. I love traveling and exploring new places.

I am an easygoing person who loves hard. I have always been that one to go the extra mile for folks, and it has often caused me a lot of heartaches. One hard lesson I learned was that not everyone has my best interest at heart. People will take advantage of you if you allow them to. Even still, I have a big heart, and I really love doing all I can to help others—even when I probably shouldn't.

Being the go to person can be a blessing or a burden, so I have to be very careful to find balance. I have always struggled to strike that balance at times, and that can be a little nerve-wracking. In recent years, I have grown in that area, and for that, I am proud of myself.

I am a fairly quiet person who can talk your ear off about things I am passionate about. I enjoy books, webinars, seminars, classes, and any other media as an avenue to learn and grow. I love all things natural health and wellness. I am a Certified Health Specialist, and a Certified Authentic Essential Oils Specialist. I am the owner/CEO of Serenity Health and Wellness.

I am an author who loves reading, writing, and researching just about anything interesting. I am a people watcher. It's quite interesting to watch people and wonder what their story might be. People are quite amusing at times.

I love thrift stores, garage sales, and estate sales. The he old Westerns: *Bonanza, Big Valley, Gunsmoke, The Rifleman, Wagon Train,* and *Rawhide* are some of my favorite shows.

As a believer and follower of Jesus Christ, I endeavor to love God with all my heart, yet I know I fall short. What's most important to me is knowing that God loves me unconditionally and without measure.

I am grateful for God's unending grace and mercy toward me. Every single day I stand in awe of the greatness of God. He is my everything. I am a lover of God's Word, and I love people. I wish everyone would experience a relationship with Jesus as I have been privileged to do. I'm talking about a real, vibrant, personal relationship—not some religious ideology.

I despise every form of injustice, inequality, and hatred. Each person is created in the image of God and deserves to be treated as such.

I am a licensed and ordained minister of the Gospel. My mandate is to teach and preach the unadulterated Gospel of Jesus Christ. My heart's focus is on women. I want women to truly know and understand just how much God loves them. My mission is for them to live out that revelation. If only women knew that God is not mad at them, how profoundly different their lives could be. God does not require perfection. We are all imperfect, and God loves us anyway. It's difficult to grasp this truth in a world that demands we look and act perfect. It's impossible to meet the expectations of this world so stop trying. God is our only place of identity, safety, and security.

I want women to know their worth and never compromise who they are. I want to see women develop and cultivate their gifts not only for the glory of God but for their world, their sphere of influence. I want women to discover and fulfill their destinies.

My husband and I pastor a local church where I serve as Executive Pastor. I have served in ministry for over thirty-five years where I've witnessed the power of God displayed and lives changed. I've taught God's Word with miracles and signs following. I have laid hands on the sick and seen them recover. I have seen blind eyes opened. I have experienced healings and miracles in my own body. I have seen the spiritual gifts in operation and experienced things that cannot be explained naturally. I have spoken at conferences and conducted workshops and seminars.

I have placed my life in God's hands. I desire to please Him and be the expression of His love, grace, and mercy in this world. I have experienced God in so many amazing ways and through simple acts of His grace. I never had reason to question God's power, the authority of His Word, or His love for me.

So why am I telling you all of this? Because I want you to know that I am just a normal girl out there also trying to live her life. I'm no different than you. I have hopes and big dreams. I experience hurts, disappointments, setbacks, and I fight fear, doubt, and insecurity at times and sometimes all at the same time.

And just like some of you may have experienced, my life one day turned upside down. I found myself staring down anxiety, depression, and fear. Like formidable enemies, they came at me in full force. I was blindsided and found myself stumbling and staggering.

Before I knew it, I was questioning everything I thought and said I believed. I was experiencing what I had heard about but had never experienced—a crisis of belief. My struggle with anxiety and depression shook me to my core. Why and how could this be happening to me? My belief and my faith were being called into account.

Beneath the Surface: Unearthing the Seedbed of Anxiety and Depression allows you to peek into that moment of my life. There were many bad days, many sad days, and many hard days, yet I can now say that those days are now behind me.

You will be enlightened and empowered as you read this powerful account of my life. My journey is a story of hope and inspiration. I will share how I went from being devastated by anxiety and depression to how God led me on a journey to triumph over it. This book will serve as encouragement for anyone who suffers from anxiety and depression and for those who love someone who does.

I have exciting news. There is a wonderful life beyond anxiety and depression. I know because I *was* one of the statistics. I was hiding with overwhelming feelings of shame, guilt, and condemnation. My suffering in silence continued for years. But along my journey back to wellness, I learned and gained tremendous insight.

One day I cried out to God on my knees. He shared a vision with me of women all over the world doing the exact same thing. Some were prostrate on the floor. All of them were crying and asking God for help. I immediately realized that I was not alone. I yelled out to God that "when" He helped me through to the other side of anxiety and depression, I would do whatever I could to help others. I promised God that I would use what I've learned to help other women, and *now* is that time!

I will share my personal and painful testimony to dispel some myths about anxiety and depression. I will expose the stigma leading to shame, guilt, and condemnation. I am speaking to all women, yet I am more specifically speaking to women in ministry and women of color. Women in ministry have unique challenges already, and I want to help you navigate those challenges.

I want to speak to women of color because there are cultural differences; Cultural and societal-held beliefs and expectations complicate this issue. To the women of color in ministries, well ladies, hold on because we have a lot to cover. My sincere hope in sharing my story is to educate, encourage, and empower you along this journey we call *life*.

I want to speak to the Church at large by challenging my brothers and sisters in Christ to reevaluate how those suffering from anxiety, depression, and/or any other mental or emotional challenge have been traditionally viewed and treated. The Bible teaches you to pursue understanding, so I will do my best to help you understand.

Anxiety and depression are real. They are just as real as any other diagnosis. You may not struggle with anxiety or depression, but I absolutely know that someone you know does. So I implore you to have an open mind about this serious and complex issue so you can potentially educate and help someone else. In sharing my story, I will unearth the seedbed (the root causes) of anxiety and depression and, with that understanding, promote healing and wholeness.

Now that I've introduced myself to you and shared why I wrote this book, let me tell you the most important thing about me. I am human. You may say, "duh, of course, you are." Well, this is something I have to remind myself of often because I have been known to think that I am Wonder Woman. But life has taught me that I am not. I have a feeling that you might relate to that feeling. Well, from this flawed, yet fabulous, human to you, you are not alone, and *I understand*!

CHAPTER 2 - STRONG BLACK WOMAN

"Don't be ashamed of your story.

It will inspire others."

-Unknown

My story isn't as unique as I had initially thought. I was clueless to the fact that millions of people struggle with anxiety and depression and often without support or hope. Even more shocking was that I never imagined that this would ever happen to me. Before we get into my story, go grab a cup of tea, slip on your favorite comfy pajama's, find a quiet place to put your feet up, and relax. Go ahead and get ready. I'll be right here when you get back.

SPRING STORMS

Ready? Let me share an illustration to help you understand how my story played out. You will see just how ones' life can change in an instant.

Springtime is one of my most favorite times of the year. The days are getting longer, trees are beginning to bud, and spring flowers are emerging. The air is fresh and clean. There is a sense of renewal everywhere. This particular spring day started in its typical sunny fashion. It was gorgeous here in Central Florida. The temperature was about seventy-eight degrees, and there was a slight breeze in the air. Pure perfection —not too hot nor was it too cool.

The blue sky was kissed with the most picturesque cumulus clouds. No painting or picture could ever do these clouds justice. The depth of green on the leaves of the trees displayed health and vitality. Oh my, what a sight. The vibrant colors of the emerging flowers were so captivating. All I could do was admire the handiwork of God's creation.

Stepping into the warmth of the sun, I breathed in deeply, inhaling the fresh air. The sun felt so rejuvenating on my face. Communing with nature was simply amazing. I couldn't help but praise God for the splendor of His day. Off in the distance, I could hear a chorus of birds singing their little hearts out. It was music to my ears. I believe they, too, were praising God for the beauty of this moment. I sat in my favorite patio chair. It was a most precious time— resting in the peace and tranquility of the day. Wow, who could ever say that there is no God? How could anyone look around and doubt the existence of a Creator? The very creation—the sun, clouds, and birds—all speak of His Glory.

After some time, I went back inside to get a drink and check on a few things. As I looked back outside, the blue skies had turned a bit gray. In just a few minutes more, I noticed that the wind had started blowing, followed by sheets of incessant rain. Suddenly, we were in the midst of a terrible storm with torrential rains and deafening thunder.

How does the weather turn so quickly from absolutely beautiful to absolutely dark and ugly in a matter of minutes? Welcome to Central Florida. This scenario is real. It happens just about every day here during our rainy season. Ask anyone who lives in Florida or the seventy million visitors who make Orlando Florida their vacation destination each year.

Instantly, the weather can change on us. Sometimes a torrential downpour with heavy winds and dark skies can last for a few minutes or a few hours. Then voila, here comes the sun again. However, there are times when the storm can go on for hours and even days. Eventually, it will all clear up, and we go on to enjoy our beautiful day.

THE STORMS OF LIFE

Just like natural storms, life has a way of giving rise to its own storms. The storms of life seem to come out of nowhere— suddenly and with little warning. Unlike natural storms, life doesn't come with a meteorologist to warn us of inclement weather. Life just happens—whether we are ready for it or not.

I know this because that's exactly what happened to me. Life was good and then one day, little did I know, a major thunderstorm was brewing on the inside of me.

As the skyline of my life suddenly darkened, the winds blew fiercely around me. Torrential rain poured so hard and sideways that I was temporarily blinded. I could not see my way forward. The lightning was so brilliant and beautiful as it danced from place to place; yet it, too, blinded me. As I tried to refocus my attention to see what was going on, I began to hear the thunder. Initially, it sounded far away, and I could hear a faint rumble every once in a while. Before long, the thunder was closer, and it began to get louder. All of a sudden, I began to feel the trembling effects of the thunder. Then, *boom*! The thunder was so loud, so deafening, and so strong that it shook my very being—my entire life. I was in the midst of the greatest storm of my life.

I was extremely confused because unlike the storms in Central Florida, this storm was not going away. I tried to reassure myself by saying that this "storm" going on within me will pass soon. Well, hours turned into days. Days turned into weeks. Weeks turned into months, and months turned into years. Three very long, dark, and scary years passed and took a physical, emotional, and mental toll on my life in ways I could have never imagined. Now, let me explain.

THE PERFECT STORM

In 2009, Darryl and I were extremely excited to be moving to the Sunshine State. Orlando was always our favorite vacation destination. We visited often with our children spending days running from one amusement park to another. There was always something extra special about Florida. The skies seemed bluer, and the clouds appeared to be whiter and fluffier. I felt alive in Florida. I loved the beautiful palm trees. Florida felt like home. At the end of every vacation, I was never ready to leave. Darryl and I both felt a strange connection to Florida and never quite understood why.

Darryl had shared with me that God had called him to eventually plant a church in Orlando. We weren't sure when, but we would be ready when the time came. A few years passed, and Darryl was relocated to Tampa by his employer. God, is this the time we've been waiting on?

Yes, it was *go* time! Can you imagine how thrilled we were? It was exciting and just as scary. We didn't have family or friends in the Tampa area, but we had a lot of faith and a big vision. This was going to be a tremendous walk of faith, and we were ready. At least, we thought we were. We knew that God was leading, and we were ready to follow knowing that He would direct our every step.

We had two weeks—yes, two weeks to schedule a move and get to Florida. It was full steam ahead. We put our house on the market and scheduled the movers. I scoured the real estate listings looking for a place to live. We eventually rented a home in Winter Haven, Florida, between Tampa and Orlando. After we settled in Winter Haven, we spent our weekends praying, driving around Orlando with a map, and asking God to show us where to plant this church.

All of this excitement was coming on the heels of Darryl retiring after twenty-five years in the Air Force. Our daughter, Kristian, was attending Florida State University, and our son, Brandon was working and living in Tallahassee.

LIFE HAPPENS

Back in my hometown of Hendersonville, North Carolina, things with my mother were not going well. She had been diagnosed with lung cancer. She had undergone surgery and chemotherapy treatments. We were told that the cancer was gone. My mother had recovered well enough to attend our son's wedding in Virginia. I was so overjoyed to see her out on the dance floor cutting the rug. All was well. Or so we thought.

During this same time, a dear friend in the Virginia/DC area had recently been diagnosed with cancer. She started chemotherapy immediately, and the treatments were abruptly stopped. She was too weak to continue. Her husband called and told me that she was dying. Darryl and I flew to Virginia to find her curled up in a hospital bed. My heart dropped; she was already a small woman. She was so tiny, bald, and in a fetal position. As I fought back tears, I reached out and took her hand. As I called her name, she began to stir. She tried to open her eyes and move her mouth. She was too weak. As I spoke to her, machines began beeping and ringing. The nurse said to me, "She knows you're here, and she is trying to communicate." Darryl and I prayed for her. We sat with her for hours as she was in and out of consciousness. We kissed her and left believing she would recover. A few days later, her husband called. She had transitioned peacefully. I was heartbroken.

Darryl and I are back in Florida moving forward with the church. Planting a church is a real struggle. It's truly a calling and no one in their right mind would want to do this unless they are called. It was much harder than we ever imagined. It is definitely not for the faint of heart!

I started noticing I wasn't feeling well. I was tired. My stomach hurt, and I attributed it to eating on the run and not being as healthy as I should have been. One morning, I woke up feeling shaky and wondered what was going on. I didn't have much of an appetite either, so I decided to see a doctor. My doctor prescribed a few different medications, but nothing seemed to work.

Over the next months, my digestive problems grew worse. I was referred to a gastroenterologist. He diagnosed me with gastroesophageal reflux disease. He prescribed one medication after another. I couldn't eat much of anything without my stomach pain or nausea. I lost a lot of weight. I wasn't sleeping.

After more testing, my gastroenterologist prescribed Reglan to treat what he diagnosed as gastroparesis. I noticed a "black box warning" sticker on the bottle. I searched Dr. Google and discovered that there was an active lawsuit pending against this medication. It was reported to cause tardive dyskinesia, a disorder where parts of your body move involuntarily, and those movements might not stop even when the medication is discontinued.

I called the doctor. He told me that this side effect is rare, and he's only seen it happen in a few patients. I disagreed with him based on the research I had done. He instructed me to just take the medication and see if it would help. I told him I would not take the chance. I asked him why he would prescribe a medication with a pending lawsuit against it. He insisted that it's not as bad as it has been reported. I asked if he would prescribe it to his wife or daughter. He wouldn't answer me. His silence was my answer.

I was given a referral to a new gastroenterologist who reviewed my test results and told me that I had been misdiagnosed. I didn't have gastroparesis after all. I was upset and was back to square one with my digestive problems.

In the midst of all of this, I was having private summers. Ladies, you know exactly what I mean: menopausal symptoms. I was hot and sweaty on top of everything else that was happening to my body.

Early one morning, I woke up nauseous and sick. I head to the bathroom. I felt like I was shaking on the inside. I was breathing heavily, sweating, and crying as I fell to the floor. I couldn't breathe. I felt like I was going to die. It seemed like an eternity before I could move. I called Darryl and realized he wasn't allowed to have his phone while at work. I sat there praying and wondering what the heck just happened. I contemplated calling 911, but just like that, I was feeling better. I had these "episodes" a few more times in the next few days. I did not understand what was happening. I had made an appointment to see my doctor the following week.

PANIC ATTACKS

Saturday morning rolled around. I asked Darryl to take me to the emergency room because the "episodes" were happening back-to-back, and I could not wait until next week. I was crying uncontrollably, and I felt like someone was standing on my chest. I was shaking. It felt like my body was "thundering." I have no other way to describe what I was experiencing. Have you ever felt thunder shake your house? That's what I was feeling on the inside. I was terrified because I had no idea what was going on.

At the emergency room, I was still crying as a female doctor walks in. My breathing was still labored, and my blood pressure was elevated. She explains that I am having a panic attack. I'm like, what? She hands me an itty-bitty little pill to calm me down. I took the pill and laid back on the bed. I was rocking back and forth and praying. I felt confused and embarrassed. What is wrong with me? How could this be? I'm a woman of God, a woman of *great faith. A strong black woman.*

Within minutes of taking that itty-bitty little pill, I was as chill as a cucumber. The thundering stopped, and I felt at peace. The doctor reappeared again to check on me. I explained to her what I have been experiencing, and again, she stated, "You are having panic attacks." She went on to explain that panic attacks are extremely common. She stated that she sees it in the emergency room every day. She sent me home to follow up with my primary care doctor.

On the ride home, I felt so embarrassed and ashamed. I was wondering, what is Darryl thinking? I was wondering, how can this be happening to me? I closed my eyes and put my head down in my lap and cried. Darryl's hand caressed my back. I heard him talking to me, but I don't even know what he said. I was exhausted: physically and mentally. I just wanted to go home and climb back in bed.

I finally saw my doctor. He concluded that I was probably under a lot of pressure. He wrote me a prescription for Ativan (the same itty-bitty little pill). I tried to tell him about the "thundering" I felt on the inside, but he just stared at me.

I pick up the prescription for Ativan. It did help but it did not prevent panic attacks. It only shortened the duration of the panic attacks. As time went on, I began to have panic attacks more often. I still had no answer for the other symptoms I was experiencing, and I was quite annoyed.

BACK TO LIFE

I was perplexed. I was trying to get back to my life, but I was still struggling. I was losing more weight, and it was evident to everyone around me. I hated how I looked and felt. I felt sick to my stomach most of the time. I couldn't eat. I couldn't sleep. I was praying and not sure what to think.

Why couldn't I shake this? Why wasn't I stronger than this? Why couldn't I get my mind together and get past this? I was watching people watch me and wondered what they were thinking. I hadn't even told Darryl how bad things were.

Most nights I would wait for Darryl to go to sleep, then I would go to another room and lay on the floor. Why the floor? I have no idea, but I would just lay there and cry because my stomach hurt so bad. I felt the constant thundering in my body, and I just could not sleep. It went on like this for a long time. I was embarrassed and ashamed.

Soon, I noticed that I was moving in slow motion. All of my actions were delayed. I was fatigued. I decided to go back to my doctor. As I sat in his office, I tried once again to explain what I was feeling. This time he looked at me and said, "You are depressed. I see it every day." I just sat there too exhausted to say anything else. He decided that I should try a drug called Lexapro. He assured me it was safe and explained that he sees amazing results in his patients. I agreed to "try" it and see him in a few weeks.

In about two weeks, I was feeling worse. Sunday morning, I woke up and noticed that my teeth and gums hurt. I had a strange taste in my mouth. I went to church and was miserable throughout the service. I went home and went to bed where I stayed until the next morning.

That Monday, I had an appointment with the gastroenterologist. I felt weak, nauseous, and disoriented. Darryl brought me breakfast, but I couldn't eat it because my teeth and gums were hurting.

While in the doctor's office scheduling a colonoscopy appointment, I began feeling light-headed. The next thing I remember is someone calling my name. I had passed out. I could hear paramedics saying that my heart rate was racing, and my breathing was labored. Next, I hear ambulance sirens as they rushed me to the hospital. I don't remember much about the ride other than feeling the sensation of the blood pressure cuff. I told the EMT it was too tight. I looked up, and he said, "It's ok, and you will be ok." I closed my eyes and whispered, "God, please help me."

I was admitted to the hospital for a week as they ran a battery of tests. They stopped the Lexapro immediately and then started me back on it a few days before I left the hospital. My teeth and gums started hurting again, and my heart started racing again. I was placed on a heart monitor until my heart rate returned to normal. My doctor was contacted, and he suggested that I give my body time to get used to the medication. I declined. No, thank you, sir. I refuse to take a medication that literally put me in this hospital bed.

Since I was already in the hospital, my gastroenterologist performed a colonoscopy. It came back fine. I was released from the hospital still experiencing digestive distress and feeling bad.

Normal tasks were becoming more difficult. Shopping, going to the grocery store, and even dealing with people was exhausting. Everything aggravated me. I couldn't stand to hear a phone ring. Avoiding people and isolating myself became the norm for me. I would stay home, read my bible, and pray. I would go to church every week and try and hold it together. I was still teaching and praying while wondering, what is wrong with me?

One weekend, Darryl and I went to an outlet mall. Normally, we synchronize our watches, go our separate ways, and meet back at a certain time. This time, I followed him around like a puppy. I didn't care to shop. I didn't feel well.

ME? DEPRESSED?

I was in bed early. Darryl came into the room and knelt by the bed. He mentioned he was getting very concerned because I was not myself. As he shared all of his concerns, I laid there crying. He said he was praying for me and saw the word "depression." I immediately got angry and told him not to say that. He told me we had to deal with what was going on. As he explained the symptoms, I realized he was right, but I didn't want to accept it. How can this be happening to me? Could the doctor be right? Maybe he had just prescribed the wrong medication. I was confused. I didn't understand. I had never experienced anything like this, and I was scared. We prayed. I cried myself to sleep.

I went back to the doctor again. He insisted that Lexapro did not cause the side effects. At this point, I didn't care. He prescribed a new medication, Celexa (Citalopram). It was supposed to be much easier to tolerate. Well, it caused me terrible nausea. I contacted his office, and he sent in a prescription for Nexium (Esomeprazole) and Phenergan (Promethazine HCl) to help with nausea. He added a prescription for Ambien to help with sleep.

At my follow-up appointment, the doctor listened as I explained that I was not better. He excused himself from the room. He returned with a prescription for Wellbutrin and tried to sell me on how it might help me. I took the prescription and left his office. I sat in my car and cried. I threw the prescription in the passenger seat and drove home. He had written six prescriptions, and I wasn't healing, and I had no answers. I was done. As I look back, I don't know why I kept going back.

THERE HAS TO BE A BETTER WAY

I was praying and asking God for guidance because something had to change. This was not working. There had to be a better way. I needed to find someone who would get to the root of what was going on with me and not just throw medication at me. I needed to find someone who believed in a holistic approach to health and wellness. I mentioned to my chiropractor that I was looking for a new doctor and why. She recommended Dr. Eudene Harry. Dr. Harry is a board-certified medical doctor. She is an African American physician who is holistic in her approach to wellness.

I made an appointment with Dr. Harry, and I was so glad I did. Dr. Harry was amazing. I talked, and she listened. What a concept. She and I talked for about an hour. I finally felt like I could breathe because she listened and took the time to try and understand. She changed my prescription of Ativan to Klonopin (clonazepam) so that it would be easier for me to wean off when it was time to discontinue the medication.

I worked with Dr. Harry for about eight months or so. She didn't take insurance, so I was paying out of pocket. She did a lot of testing and some for free. The testing revealed that my mercury levels were too high, my cortisol levels were too high, my neurotransmitters were out of whack, and some of my vitamin and mineral levels were also out of balance. We came up with a game plan to work on all of this.

Dr. Harry explained that medications cannot fix everything and that in many cases they only mask symptoms. I learned that medications do not address the root cause of the disease within the body. She was extremely knowledgeable and explained all of the medicalese to me in layman's terms. She was encouraging and empowering. It was comforting having a black female doctor I could relate to and who cared. During times when I was struggling, I could call her, and she would take the time to walk me through a rough moment. She went above and beyond to offer me support when I needed it.

She encouraged a healthier diet and supplements to help with the anxiety along with supplementation to help bring my body back into balance. She stressed the importance of resting —something I needed to do.

I was starting to feel better, but I was still not back to my old self. I was feeling depressed, and I asked her about depression medications. She suggested a drug called Paxil (Paroxetine) for depression and to see if it would help balance my neurotransmitters. She warned that it could increase feelings of anxiety, and if it did, we would need to stop it. I began taking Paxil and started to experience increased anxiety, so I stopped taking it as she had said.

I AM LOSING IT

Weeks later, I was becoming very restless and agitated. One morning, I walked into the kitchen where Darryl was eating breakfast. I felt like I was losing my mind. I was crying and screaming because I felt like I could not go on like this. I was leaning against the wall, and I began sliding down the wall sobbing. Darryl tried to comfort me and tell me everything would be ok. I was so tired of hearing that. I jumped up, ran over, and grabbed a huge knife, and put it to my wrist saying, "I know how to make it ok." Darryl wrestled the knife out of my hand. I fell back to the floor crying and sobbing. I kept apologizing to him. I felt so ashamed. Was I crazy? I remember screaming, "God, what is wrong with me? Please help me!" Darryl holds me, prays with me, and rocks me in his arms until I stop crying.

He then calls Dr. Harry and explains what is happening and asks for advice about what we could do. She tells me that I needed to see someone today. Dr. Harry was able to get me in to see a psychiatrist she knew.

THE PSYCHIATRIST VISIT

I arrived at the psychiatrist's office for an evaluation. I spoke with the intake specialist and completed some paperwork. She went and talked with the doctor. She returned and ushered us into the office. We sat there in silence. The doctor is sitting with his face inches from his computer screen and fumbling through my papers. Several minutes go by before he looks up. He just blurts out, "This is easy. You have bipolar disease. It lays dormant and can trigger at any age. It's nothing to be ashamed of. Many famous and successful people live and strive with bipolar disease. We have very effective medications to treat bipolar disease, so once we get you on the right medication, you can live a wonderful and productive life."

Wow! I'm sitting there in complete shock. I'm bipolar? What? I heard his words, but somehow, they were not computing. How could this be? Immediately, I thought, *no way*! Was that just pride and fear? The doctor went on to explain bipolar disease, and all I heard from that point was blah, blah, blah!

He hands me a prescription for Risperidone (Risperdal). I left wondering, what has become of my life? God, what is going on? I am praying, and I am trusting you, but this is ridiculous. I am so embarrassed. I have just been diagnosed with bipolar disease. What the heck? I am trying to make sense of all of this. I was so desperate for relief that I honestly think I would have tried something illegal at this point.

I start taking the medication and within a few weeks, I began to feel better. My energy levels had increased, and for once, in a long time, I felt pretty good. I was still having some digestive issues, but at least I felt better. So maybe the doctor was right. Who has to know about this diagnosis? As he said, some great people we all know and love have bipolar disease. I guess it is what it is. I will just have to deal with it.

Yes, I am feeling better. *Then* one afternoon, I started feeling extremely anxious, and I literally could not sit down. I was crying and pacing the floor while rubbing my arms and legs over and over. That "thundering" feeling was echoing through my whole body louder than ever. I was shaking and trembling. Fear started settling in because I didn't know what was going on.

I called the doctor's office, and they instructed me to stop the medication immediately and come in for an assessment. According to the doctor, my body had built a tolerance quickly, and he needed to increase the dosage, and my body would adjust and then stabilize. He increased the dosage and sent me on my way.

Within another week or so, I was having a similar episode. It's happening all over again. I was having bad mood swings. I was raging over everything. I began having unrelenting thoughts of suicide and death.

HERE WE GO AGAIN

This time, the doctor's office insisted I stop the
Risperidone. Darryl is instructed to take me to the local
Behavioral hospital if he felt it was necessary. By this point, I
was ready to go because I was afraid I might hurt myself. I was
scared, and my hope was that they would keep me for
evaluation and give me something so I could rest and sleep. I
felt like I was on the edge of losing my mind.

OFF TO THE BEHAVIORAL HOSPITAL

I arrived at a local behavioral hospital. I sat in a cold,
dark, waiting area. I remember pulling my arms up into my
shirt sleeves. I didn't see anyone but the receptionist and she
didn't seem too happy herself. I didn't know what to expect. It
was pretty scary. They finally performed their intake and
assessment. Yes, you have signs of anxiety and depression, but
we see no reason to keep you here. They asked if I would
consider participating in their outpatient program. I would
receive personalized counseling, group counseling, and classes.
I would come in daily and participate in sessions as long as I
wanted. Darryl and I talked it over, prayed about it, and felt it
might be helpful.

The first day I show up for the outpatient program, I pull the first door open and walk into the building. I reach for the next door to find it locked. An attendant looked up and buzzed me in. I showed her my identification and signed in. I then met with the coordinator who explained the program and gave me some insight into what to expect and how to navigate in the sessions—the rules and things.

She then walked me to my appointment with the psychiatrist. I was extremely nervous. I shared all that I had been going through, including the medications I was on and had been on. I explained how I had experienced bad reactions to some previous medications. I answered his questions. He answered my questions. We talked for some time, and he told me that he did *not* agree with the bipolar disease diagnosis. He said, "I don't see that Mrs. Marjorie, but I do see the anxiety and depression, so let's work on that."

He increased the Klonopin to help with the anxiety and added Trazadone to help with depression and sleep since I was still dealing with insomnia. I was hesitant because of what I had recently experienced, but he assured me that it just takes time to find the right combination of medications and that this combination works very well. We finish our session, and he tells me to go to the group therapy session, hang in there, and I would be just fine.

GROUP THERAPY

I walk into the group therapy class that was already in session. I find a seat in the circle. I look around at each person wondering why they were here. As I listened to men and women of all ages and races share their stories, I could do nothing but cry. I never knew much about mental illness. I just sat there listening. The sad faces, the sad stories, and the tears flowing everywhere were more than I could take. I was so emotionally overwhelmed. Why and how am I here?

One by one, the therapist called on each person around the circle. Some shared while others just curled up in their chairs and said nothing. Some were sleeping. A few were being disruptive. When it was my turn, I told them my name, but I couldn't say any more than that. I felt like an elephant was in my throat. I could not believe what I was seeing and hearing. I could not believe I was sitting in this room. I was so very sad. I could not wait for the day to end so I could go home.

As I was preparing to leave at the end of the day, I saw attendants come into the room. The group members lined up in different lines. I soon realized that they were there to escort them back to their rooms. As I signed out at the front desk and walked through the door, I heard the door lock behind me. I cannot explain the visceral response I had. It sent chills throughout my whole body. Tears began running down my face.

By the time I got to my car, I was in a full cry. I sat there for a moment feeling so bad for those in the group. I felt so disgusted at myself for walking in there like I was somehow better than they were. I drove home crying and repenting to God for my attitude. I could not believe that this was my life.

The next day I went in and told the group that I owed them all an apology. I told them the ugly truth of how I felt like I did not belong there because I was a pastor, a pastor's wife, blah, blah, blah, and that I was sorry for looking down my nose at them. I broke down crying. Some of them were crying too, and one by one, they all came and offered hugs. They offered such love and grace. I was so humbled by this experience. I thanked them all for understanding and accepting my apology. I made a few friends over the next three weeks I was there.

During those weeks, I learned how common mental illness is. Our classes included teachings on the different types of mental illness and their symptoms. I learned that many of the people in my group had no family support. It became very clear that their families had no understanding of what they were going through. They were scared. I realized how blessed I was to have the support of my husband and my children.

I sat with people who were hearing voices and talking to the air. I listened to horror stories of trauma and abuse. I also noticed that many of the women's stories sounded like mine. A storm had hit their lives as well, and now they were asking, "How did I get here?" I started wondering if there was something to all of this.

There were a few ladies who gravitated to me and would give me big hugs every day. We would talk and share during break time. I had the privilege of even praying for some of them. One young black girl in particular, who was always quiet and to herself, began to sit a bit closer. Before long, she would talk to me. The therapist noticed and told me that I was a light to these women. Strangely, these women were a light for me. They accepted me and treated me with respect, even after my poor attitude in the beginning.

These were some of the nicest people I had ever met. They were just people having a difficult time. I can say that I enjoyed the sessions, the classes, and my new friends. Spending time with them gave me such compassion and empathy. More importantly, it is what they gave me. I could freely talk about what I was experiencing without fear of judgment and rejection.

TIME TO LEAVE THE GROUP

Before my graduation from the program, it was required that I find a psychiatrist to continue with treatment. I was referred to a new psychiatrist in my area. They set up the appointment, and I was to see her at least once so there would be a continuum of care.

The new psychiatrist wanted me to start a whole new protocol. She felt that I would fare better with a combination of Prozac/Sarafem and Zyprexa/Olanzapine. She had already called it in at the pharmacy, and she wanted me to pick it up as soon as possible. She explained how the drugs worked and how this time would be the charm. How many times have I heard that before?

As you already know, I was already on an increased dosage of Klonopin and Trazadone. For a few weeks, I had been plugging along. I was attending the group sessions and classes, and I was intrigued by what I was learning. But I was still not feeling quite right.

NOT AGAIN

Before bed one night, I felt the "thundering" return to my body, getting louder and louder. By now, you can probably guess what happened next. The same thing that keeps happening. Another episode. I am again feeling intense anxiety. I'm shaking and crying. I take a Klonopin, and nothing happens.

As the night goes on, the anxiety worsens. I am crying and rolling all over the bed. I can't be still. I feel like running away. I feel an overwhelming urge to run. I jump up out of bed and run to the garage. I jump in my car. I head out to… I did not know where I was headed to. Darryl headed out behind me in his car. I am screaming at the top of my lungs for God to help me or just let me die. I got down the road, and I hear *go home*. It was so loud. I knew it was God. I was screaming and asking God to help me. I turn around in the middle of the street. I pass Darryl on the way back home.

I pull into the garage. I run upstairs and run into my closet. Now I'm feeling embarrassed and stupid. I felt weird. I could not feel my body. This is crazy. I couldn't calm down. I run downstairs and take another Klonopin; it doesn't help. I run back upstairs and sit in my closet crying uncontrollably. Darryl comes and sits with me in the closet.

Darryl is praying and trying to console me. I look up at him, and he looks so sad. I feel so bad for him. He doesn't deserve this. I keep apologizing. He tells me to stop apologizing because this is not my fault. At this point, I'm thinking how his life would be so much better if I were dead. I am considering just taking all the pills I have and be done with all of this. I am just done.

Darryl calls the behavioral hospital. I am crying and screaming trying to explain to the nurse what is going on with me. She asks a million questions and then asks me to come in for an evaluation. I agree to come in. I asked Darryl to take me and let them keep me until we figure out what is wrong. He says, "no." No? I get so angry. I'm yelling at him. I'm begging him to commit me, but he won't take me in. I keep telling him that I want them to give me something…anything to just knock me out for a few days. I keep insisting. He kept saying, "You do not need to be committed. It's the medicine. It's the medicine."

He kept saying, "Let's pray, wait, and see what God says." I was still thinking, maybe I'll just go ahead and take all of these freaking pills laying around this house. I will just go to sleep and never wake up. I'm so frustrated. I try to get my keys to drive myself, and he takes them away from me.

I am sitting on the floor screaming for God to help me. Darryl is trying to hug me, but I push him away. I am so tired of trying to believe and hold on. I keep telling him and God that I just can't keep taking these "episodes" anymore. I have no more strength, and I have no more fight left. I'm physically, emotionally, and mentally drained. I cannot take this!

BACK TO THE BEHAVIORAL HOSPITAL

As I sit there, I start calming down. Darryl is holding me and praying. Then just like that, he says, "Let's go." We arrive at the behavioral hospital hours later. As we check in, the nurse says, "I can see that you are calm now, and I'm glad. If you had come in when I talked to you, I would have had to Baker Act you." In other words, they would have had to keep me there.

She asked me a few questions and then told me that she believes that I was reacting to the medication but only the doctor could verify it. I was instructed not to take it anymore.

Later that morning, the psychiatrist came in and called me to his office. He pulled up his chair and looked me square in my eyes and said, "No more. You don't need these medications. For some people, these medications simply do not work. I cannot in good faith prescribe you any more medications knowing your past reactions." I told him about the other psychiatrist's protocol, and he shook his head no. "I don't think you need this, Mrs. Marjorie." He went on to tell me that he had looked at the therapist's notes, and he felt like I should continue with the classes if I thought they were helpful.

He told me to continue with the Klonopin and go back and see my doctor. I was crying at this point, and he put his hand on my back and told me to cast all my cares on Christ and everything would be okay. I looked up, and he smiled at me as he walked out of the room.

I did just as the good doctor ordered. I continued the group sessions. I did not go back to see the new psychiatrist and surely didn't take her protocol. Soon I realized that it was time to move on from the group. It was time for me to let them know that I was ready to leave.

GRADUATION DAY

On my graduation day, each person in group therapy was given the opportunity to say something to me. One by one, they all shared words of encouragement. The young black girl told me I made her feel safe and hopeful. She told me that my presence brought calm to the room, and it helped her want to attend group sessions. Each person offered kind and caring words. Of course, I was a crying mess as I listened. I was overwhelmed with love and compassion.

I was so thankful for all the love and support I was shown and for my little celebration. I realized there was a purpose in me being there, and it was bigger than me. I sensed that somehow God would not allow this experience to be wasted.

SO WHERE DO I GO FROM HERE?

I did not want to go back to the same doctors, so I found a new primary care provider. Dr. Marissa Magsino was a referral whom I had heard great things about. At my first appointment, we discussed what had been going on. I shared with her that I was working with Dr. Harry. And guess what? She knew Dr. Harry. They were friends, so we all worked together to get me going in the right direction.

Dr. Magsino also managed a private Women's Wellness business where she focused on the importance of hormonal balance. In previous years, I had hormonal panels done to determine my hormone levels. She used the same company I had used, so we decided to complete a new hormonal panel and compare the results. The results came back, and we were both amazed at how out of balance my hormones were.

TEST RESULTS

She ran a few other tests, and when all of the results were in, they revealed that I had adrenal hypofunction/fatigue, glucose intolerance, hormonal imbalance, low progesterone, menopause, high cortisol along with insomnia, anxiety, and depression. What a combination! I was a mess but now it's starting to make sense.

She explained how hormones work, and because I had a partial hysterectomy, my poor body was thrown into medical menopause. My body has been trying to balance itself but to no avail. She said, "No wonder you're having a difficult time these days." We started down the road to balancing the hormones as Dr. Harry was helping with some of the other things.

ANOTHER STORM IS BREWING

I got a call that my mother was not doing well. The cancer had spread. After the radiation treatments, she grew worse. I flew to North Carolina. She improved after a few days. I flew back to my home with plans to return soon. Not even two weeks later, I get a call that hospice has given her hours to live. I take an emergency flight back to North Carolina.

A few nights later, she took a turn for the worse. My dad was in the bed holding her as they look into one another's eyes. I was holding her hand as she took her last breath. The hospice nurse confirmed the death of my mother. It was one of the most perplexing and conflicting moments of my life. I was not ready for her to leave, but I wanted her suffering to stop. I held her hand to my face and cried. The day I so dreaded is here. I felt like I could hardly breathe. I felt like someone just punched me in the stomach.

My dad closes her eyes. I leaned over, kissed her face, and said, "I love you, mama." I was devastated. Losing my mother has been one of the most traumatic events in my life. This is the woman with whom I was bonded since my conception. She was my best friend ever. I cannot explain the bond. Nothing in life prepared me for this moment.

DISTURBING NEWS

A few days after the funeral, I was talking with some relatives and learned that my mother had stage four cancer from the beginning. Why didn't I know this? Why didn't anyone tell me this? I was so confused and hurt.

When I asked my dad, he confirmed that she did not want me to know. Darryl and I had recently started the church in Orlando, Florida, and she didn't want me running back and forth to see her. She had sworn my dad to secrecy about what was going on with her. I was so upset. I felt betrayed. Why didn't someone tell me the truth? I could have come home and spent more time with her, and no one thought about that.

I was angry. I was trying to deal with my mother's death and the circumstances surrounding some of the treatments she endured. I had all these mixed-up emotions. It was difficult processing it. I was struggling. I was angry with my family members. I was angry with my mother. I was feeling guilty for being angry at her.

The anxiety, emotional distress, panic attacks, and digestive issues were still there. I was still trying to preach, teach, and help everyone else when I could barely keep my head above water. I'm trying to be a strong black woman, and I'm bleeding out.

MAYBE IT'S TIME FOR COUNSELING/THERAPY

At this point, I remembered the words of Dr. Harry. At one appointment, I was sharing with her that I was having a difficult time coping with my mother's death and so many different things in this season of my life. She pulled up a chair and shared about a loss in her family that had taken her a long time to process. She shared how she sought the help of a therapist, and it was very helpful during that season of her life. She asked if I had ever considered talking to a therapist. I didn't say anything. But as I listened to her talk about the benefits of a therapist, a seed was sown. I wasn't convinced it was something I would do, but I appreciated her sharing her experience. I walked away thinking about how this beautiful, successful, black, female doctor went to a therapist and says she believes everyone needs a therapist. The thought was interesting, empowering, and scary.

The more I thought and prayed about it, the more I realized I needed to see a therapist to help me process all of the crap I was dealing with. I told Darryl I wanted to see a therapist. He was very supportive and encouraged me to do whatever I needed to do for my well-being. He reassured me of his love and support and that we would get through this. Just knowing I had his support made a world of difference.

It took me going through three different therapists to find Dr. Sharon Thetford. She was the real deal. She told me from day one that she wanted us to work together to get me out of her office. She was straightforward, and I loved that. She let me know that therapy was hard, emotional work, and I needed to be willing to face it straight on for it to be effective. I understood and was ready to do just that.

BACK-TO-BACK STORMS

During all of this chaos, Darryl's employer downsized, and guess what? Yes, Darryl, along with several other employees, were caught up in the corporate restructuring. One day you have a job, and then, through no fault of your own, you don't. You go from a six-figure salary to zilch. During this time, there is a government hiring freeze so finding a job in the government is impossible. No one seemed to be hiring. Despite Darryl's education, skills, and years of experience, "He couldn't buy a job," as they say. It was just one more thing to have to cope with—another storm within my storm.

Thank God for his retirement from the Air Force and for the other sources of income we had at that time. Can you imagine the stress of watching your savings decrease every month, not knowing how and when that bleeding would stop? Darryl was not taking a salary or allowances from the church at this time, so we had to trust God with this storm as well.

We were also facing church and family challenges. It was a very rough time. All I can say is, just know that God was faithful, and He came through for us like He always does.

"Each time he said, 'My grace is all you need. My power works best in weakness.' So now I am glad to boast about my weaknesses so that the power of Christ can work through me. That's why I take pleasure in my weaknesses, and in the insults, hardships, persecutions, and troubles that I suffer for Christ. For when I am weak, then I am strong" (2 Cor. 12:9–10 NLT).

Chapter 3 - Under The Influence

"The person who takes medication must recover twice. Once from the disease and once from the medication."

-William Osler

DISCLAIMER: I am in no way against the pharmaceutical industry or any medication(s). I believe that medication has its place and is necessary when it is necessary. I understand that millions of people derive benefits from medications. I understand that many people must take medications to survive. I also understand that many people have been harmed by medications.

I am simply sharing *my personal experience and opinions*. I am not suggesting that people should not take medication nor am I encouraging anyone to discontinue their medication. What I am doing is encouraging everyone to do their due diligence before taking any medication. Read the insert included with the prescription. Research the medication.

I encourage you to take responsibility for your health. Ask questions and make sure your medical professional answers your questions sufficiently. Use your voice. It's your body, your choice. Don't be afraid to find another medical professional if necessary.

Be sure the benefit of the medication outweighs the risk. In my case, it was not worth it. It was not what I needed, and it took me a long time to recover from the ill effects of the medication. I have taken medication since my encounter with certain medications and *I will* take medication again if I deem it necessary.

I learned the hard way to become my own health advocate and take responsibility for my health. I cannot and will never blindly follow any medical professional. I would encourage you to find a medical professional who is holistic in his/her approach. Medication is not always the answer, but it can be part of the answer. I've always believed that God placed everything in this world we need, including foods and herbs for our healing. I understand there are instances when we all may need medications. For instance, if I'm in excruciating pain, please give me pain medication. A carrot will not do.

MY MEDICATION MAYHEM

Let's face the truth. Medications are powerful man-made chemical compounds created in a lab. They are not natural, and they are foreign to the body. They can be toxic to the body and that explains why there are side effects.

I want to explain more about the medications I took and how they affected me. The two medications I was on the longest were Ativan and Klonopin. Of the two, I was on Klonopin the longest. Klonopin is an itty-bitty little pill, but it is quite powerful. It is classified as a Benzodiazepine.

LET'S TALK ABOUT BENZOS

Benzodiazepines referred to simply as "benzos" are a class of psychoactive drugs prescribed to treat and anxiety and insomnia. They are tranquilizers. Some of the most prescribed and most popular are Xanax (alprazolam), Ativan (lorazapem), Valium (diazapem), Klonopin (clonazepam), and Restoril (temazepam). These drugs are depressants. They are used to treat seizures, agitation, muscle spasms, panic attacks, and sedation before surgery as well.

This class of medications has been generally viewed as safe and effective for short-term use. They are intended to be taken for two to four weeks. Side effects can cause aggression, panic, and agitation. You may experience the opposite effect of what the medication is supposed to do. Benzos are also associated with an increased risk of suicidal ideation and suicide. Trust me, *I understand* exactly.

The following is a list of side effects that I experienced:

1. A constant metallic taste in my mouth
2. Fatigue
3. Tremors
4. Low/no sex drive
5. Irrational thinking
6. Loss of appetite
7. Insomnia
8. Nausea/queasiness
9. Sensitivity to sounds
10. Crying spells
11. Restlessness
12. Suicidal thoughts
13. Depression
14. Rage/anger
15. Rocking
16. A sense of moving in slow motion

Yep, all of that. There was no informed consent when I was prescribed this medication. No doctor ever told me that this medication "may" cause any of this. One day, I picked up a refill of Klonopin. There was a warning label across the top of the bottle. I didn't remember seeing it before. It included a warning and instructions to contact your medical provider if you begin experiencing rage, anger, increased anxiety, depression, or suicidal thoughts.

Well, *bingo*!!! I was experiencing all of this! Is this medication causing me more problems than it's worth? Was this medication causing the *depression*? Well, guess what? I pulled out the insert in the package and read it. Voila! Whoop, there it is! Klonopin can cause depression. It's all coming together. It wasn't until after I started taking this medication that I started experiencing depression. I'm not saying it was the only factor, but I'm confident it was a contributing factor.

KLONOPIN INSERT

In each prescription, there is a medication guide. This particular insert tells you about side effects (Genentech 2010): the possibility of suicidal thoughts/dying, possible harm to unborn babies, insomnia, panic attacks, irritability, restlessness, new or worse depression, new or worse anxiety, acting on dangerous impulses, slowing of thinking and motor skills, other unusual changes in behavior and mood, being aggressive, being angry, and/or violent. It also states the most common side effects include drowsiness, problems with walking and coordination, dizziness, depression, fatigue, and problems with memory. Then it further states, "These are not all the possible side effects of Klonopin."

Please find this Genentech insert at this website: https:// www.accessdata.fda.gov/drugsatfda_docs/label/ 2010/017533s046s048,020813s006s007medguide.pdf

This insert was an eye-opening and scary revelation. But what was I to do? I was perplexed because I couldn't just stop the medication. So I decided to do my homework to see what I had gotten myself into by taking this medication.

After about four weeks on benzos, the risk of physical dependence increases. Once the body and brain become dependent, it's much more difficult to come off of the medication.

In recent years, "benzos" have come under tremendous scrutiny because they are prescribed so freely and seemingly without much consideration of the possible harmful side effects. Long-term use of these medications has been linked to memory loss, dementia, and even cancer. There are concerns about the safety of pregnant women and the effects on children born to them.

On October 6, 2019, Cable News Network (CNN) televised a program, "This is Life with Lisa Ling: The Benzo

Crisis." It states, "Lisa Ling delves into the world of benzodiazepine use and covers the troubling threat these drugs pose when used long term and the challenges facing patients who try to quit" (Ling 2019). I would encourage you to find this episode and watch it. It confirmed everything I learned the hard way about these medications and the negative impact they can have.

Lisa shared her father's personal story by documenting his torturous experience with benzos. She filmed him in the hospital bed shaking and debilitated. The program shared some heart-wrenching stories of people suffering and some whose family members died because doctors failed to understand the gravity of the side effects of what these medications can cause.

Benzos have a long list of side effects. Here is a more complete list: drowsiness, dizziness, weakness, unsteadiness, a feeling of depression, loss of orientation, headache, sleep disturbance, confusion, irritability, aggression, excitement, memory impairment, physical dependence, trouble concentrating, blurred vision, stomach upset, nausea, low libido, increased risk of suicidal/homicidal behavior, increased anxiety, slurred speech, and the possibility of an increased risk for dementia.

Weaning off of benzos can be very difficult. Please don't attempt to do so without medical supervision. It took me a whole year to wean off. Withdrawal symptoms can include increased anxiety and panic, agitation and restlessness, tremors, dizziness, fatigue, sleep problems, shortness of breath, sweating, muscle cramps, seizures, hallucinations, stomach problems, headaches, and muscle pains. If the withdrawal isn't done correctly, one could suffer a heart attack, stroke, or even die.

Darryl did more research and found an article that helped us figure out how to slowly wean off the medication when it was time. It's called the Ashton Study (Ashton 2001). It's a twelve-year study on Benzos dependence and how to withdraw safely. I encourage you to look up Dr. Heather Ashton, a British psychopharmacologist and physician. Her manual entitled *Benzodiazepines: How They Work and How to Withdraw* (also known as The Ashton Manual) is a gold mine of information. Her goal was to shine a light on benzodiazepine dependence. It was a lifesaver for me.

A DIVINE APPOINTMENT

One day, I walked into what I thought was a health food store. I was determined not to take any more medications. I wanted off of Klonopin and felt there had to be a natural way.

As I looked around, I was greeted by Pam Wesley. She asked how she could help me. I realized that this store was actually a health and wellness business, so I explained my mistake. She then asked if I was looking for anything in particular. Don't ask me why I told her all of my business, but before I knew it, I had spilled my guts. I explained I was seeing a therapist and on medication to help with anxiety. I told her I had digestive issues. I went on to say that I didn't want to be on medications and was therefore looking for something natural to help. She looked at me and said, "I can help you." I just stared at her. I was taken aback, and I stopped in my tracks. She was so sure of herself and something about her put me at ease.

She began explaining what she does and offered me a free consultation. It all sounded great, but at this point, I'm leery to say the least. We talked for a bit, and she explained her holistic approach to wellness and how she helps clients restore health naturally. She explained she is a Christian, and she approaches what she does with prayer, and she wanted me to know that up front. We talked for a few more minutes, and I told her I would get back to her.

I wanted to see Pam and hear her out, but I was nervous. I had been praying: God, is this the direction? I felt like it was, so I went to see Pam. I have worked with Pam for years now. What I love about her is that she is always learning and sharing. She knows more than most of the doctors I've had over the years.

Her approach is holistic, and that is what I love. It includes faith in God, prayer, a healthy diet, exercise, supplementation, and self-care. She understands that every illness and problem has a root cause, and there is where she focuses.

Our first discovery was that all of my digestive issues were due to a parasitic infection that was causing an imbalance in my gut flora. Yes, nasty parasites. So we began the work of getting all of that cleaned up. I did not know that parasitic infections are extremely common and overlooked by most allopathic/western doctors. Parasites eat your food, destroy your gut flora (good bacteria), and can make you sick. Since you're not getting the proper nutrition, your health can suffer in numerous ways.

The digestive system is key to health—physical and mental. The first thing Pam does is check gut health because it is crucial to get that in check first. I incorporated digestive enzymes and probiotics into my diet. We used other supplements to support my body systems. We began a protocol to get my nervous system calmed down and help my body come into balance.

NO MORE KLONOPIN

It came time to wean off of Klonopin. My primary care doctor, Dr. Magsino, approved and was on board. As I said, it took a year of shaving off bits of that itty-bitty pill until the day came when I felt God spoke to my heart and said, "You're good. You don't need the medication anymore." Those were the words I had been confessing over my body and mind. I would pray over my body and my brain confessing God's Word for my healing. I would take my supplements to help my body and believe that one day this would all pass.

One thing I made clear throughout this ordeal was that God is my healer, and the supplements and other modalities only help the process of healing. God can use supplements and others to help bring about my healing.

I admit I was pretty scared to go without the medication. I knew stopping the medication could cause an anxiety rebound effect and that would not be fun. I felt it was necessary to tell Darryl I was stopping the medication in case I had another "episode," but God told me, "No, this is between you and me." I was hesitant, but I decided to trust Him.

After a week of no medication, no anxiety, no panic attacks, and no depression, I walked up to Darryl and said, "Tell me congratulations." He asked why, and I told him to just say it. I told him everything, and He was overjoyed. We both cried and celebrated the goodness and delivering power of God. We prayed and gave God thanks for how He worked in and through us in so many different ways. It was a joyous day. *That was January 14, 2014! Praise God! Hallelujah!*

It was a long journey, but God was faithful as He always is. I want you to understand that healing is a process, and it can take time. God is able to make all grace abound toward us as we trust him along the way.

As I began my medication-free journey, I was so happy to finally feel normal again. It was an amazing feeling. Everything seemed brighter and lighter. I had my life back, and I was so grateful to God and all the people who were a part of my journey. I had a community of people dedicated to my well-being. It seemed like a crazy and chaotic road, but it led me to this wonderful day.

I do not regret anything I've been through because I learned so much. I am now in a position to help so many others. I will never be the same, and I mean that in the best possible way!

TIME TO DETOX

It's time to detox all of the medications I had been on for three years. Medication toxins can linger in your tissues and organs for years. The process of detoxification was pretty tough at times, and we had to adjust and readjust supplements because my body had been through so much, and it was overly sensitive. There were times when I could smell the medications leaving my body. Smelly, but necessary. We took it one day at a time.

My body had been under assault for three years. Remember, I was starting and stopping anxiety and depression medications. These drugs alter the nervous system and brain chemistry.

I had also been taking all sorts of digestive medications. It was now time to detox from all the "prescription" medications. Medications are unleashed into the bloodstream and circulate throughout the entire body. Discontinuing the medication does not mean it's not still in the body.

MY SISTERS IN HEALTH

In the final months of my battle, Dr. Magsino, my primary care physician, was helping to balance my hormones, Pam was helping to detox and support my different body systems, and my amazing therapist, Dr. Sharon Thetford, was on board helping me detox from my negative thinking and helping me process what I was going through.

Others also helped along the way, and I mentioned them all upfront. In the end, all of these amazing people were my health and wholeness dream team. Each person along the way was an integral part of making my journey a successful one. I am so blessed to have had them along my journey to wellness. It was a long road full of bumps, but with God's help, I made it. I am so thankful to God for each one of them and for using them to lead and guide me along the highway to wellness as I am no longer *under the influence.*

THREE YEARS A SLAVE

For three years, I was under the influence of one medication or another. As you know, the medications for anxiety and depression were devastating for me. Most times, the side effects were worse than the initial symptoms I was experiencing.

Here is a list of the prescription medications I took at one time or another during this ordeal. *Note: This is the scary road of the "let's try this" approach that eventually led to the physical and emotional wreck I suffered.*

This list is just to help you understand what my brain and body endured during those three years.

LIST OF MEDICATIONS I TOOK

Lexapro/escitalopram—Selective Serotonin Reuptake Inhibitor (SSRI). Treats major depressive disorder/generalized anxiety disorder.

Paxil/paroxetine—Selective Serotonin Reuptake Inhibitor (SSRI). Treats major depressive disorder/generalized anxiety disorder/obsessive-compulsive disorder (OCD).

Celexa/citalopram—Selective Serotonin Reuptake Inhibitor (SSRI). Treats depression.

Ativan/lorazepam—Benzodiazepine (Sedative). Treats seizures disorders and anxiety.

Klonopin/clonazepam—Benzodiazepine (Sedative). Treats seizures, anxiety, and/or panic attacks.

Risperidone/Risperdal—Antipsychotic. Treats bipolar disorder, schizophrenia, and irritability caused by autism.

Nexium/esomeprazole—Proton-pump inhibitor. Treats gastroesophageal reflux disease (GERD).

Symax Duotab/ hyoscyamine—Anti-tremor and gut antispasmodic. Treats muscle cramps in the bowels or bladder, irritable bowel syndrome (IBS), colitis, and stomach ulcers.

Omeprazole DR/Prilosec—Proton-pump inhibitor. Treats acid reflux.

Potassium CL ER—Electrolyte. Treats low potassium levels.

Zofran/Ondansetron HCL—Antiemetic. Treats nausea and vomiting.

Phenazopyridine/Pyridium—Analgesic. Treats urinary tract infections.

Promethazine/Phenergan—Antihistamine and Antiemetic. Treats nausea and vomiting.

Pantoprazole SOD DR/Protonix—Proton-pump inhibitor. Treats gastroesophageal reflux disease (GERD).

Ambien/Zolpidem Tartrate—Sedative-hypnotic. Treats insomnia.

Ciprofloxacin Hcl/Cipro—Antibiotic. Treats infections.

Trazadone/Desyrel—Antidepressant and Sedative Serotonin antagonist and reuptake inhibitor – treat depression and insomnia.

Tramadol Hcl—Narcotic. Treats pain but is also an opioid used to treat depression.

Aciphex/rabeprazole—Proton-pump inhibitor. Treats heartburn, stomach ulcers, and gastroesophageal reflux disease (GERD).

Hyomax-DT/hyoscyamine—Anti-tremor and gut antispasmodic. Treats muscle cramps in the bowels or bladder, irritable bowel syndrome (IBS), colitis, and stomach ulcers.

LIST OF MEDICATIONS I WAS PRESCRIBED BUT DID NOT TAKE

Wellbutrin SR/bupropion—Antidepressant. Treats depression.

Zoloft/sertraline—Selective Serotonin Reuptake Inhibitor (SSRI) and antidepressant. Treats depression, obsessive-compulsive disorder (OCD), posttraumatic stress disorder (PTSD), social anxiety, and panic disorder.

Xanax/alprazolam—Benzodiazepines and sedative. Treats anxiety and panic disorder.

Prozac/Sarafem—Selective serotonin Reuptake Inhibitor (SSRI) and antidepressant. Treats depression, obsessive-compulsive disorder (OCD), bulimia nervosa, and panic disorder.

Zyprexa/olanzapine—Atypical antipsychotic. Treats mental disorders, including schizophrenia and bipolar disorder.

Reglan/metoclopramide—Dopamine antagonists, antiemetic, and Gut motility stimulator. Treats gastroesophageal reflux disease (GERD). It also treats gastroparesis in patients with diabetes. This is the medication I mentioned earlier that came with a Black Box Warning.

*Note: A Black Box Warning is the Food and Drug Administration's (FDA) most serious type of warning about injury harm or other serious life-threatening risks linked to prescription medication. In this case, it stated that taking this drug may cause tardive dyskinesia, a serious, often irreversible movement disorder. Those movements may be involuntary, repetitive, movements of the extremities, lip smacking, grimacing, tongue protrusion, rapid eye movements, or blinking, puckering, pursing of the lips, or impaired movements of the hands and feet. Parkinsonism a similar disorder to Parkinson's disease is also reported. The discontinuation of the drug may not cause the movement to go away. There are lawsuits against the manufacturers of Reglan. No, thank you!

I am so thankful to God that I survived and that I am now thriving. As I said earlier, "...I am no longer *under the influence.*" Sadly, however, many others are not so fortunate.

God was and is always faithful to His Word. One scripture I quoted daily, posted on my wall, and read often was "*I will give you back your health and heal your wounds, says the Lord*" (Jer. 30:17 NLT). And He did.

CHAPTER 4 - UNEARTHING THE SEEDBED OF ANXIETY AND DEPRESSION

"Look beneath the surface so you can judge

correctly."

-John 7:24 NLT

Anxiety and depression are both extremely common and are becoming increasingly more common in our society. Teens and young children are being diagnosed at alarming rates. Since there are many causes of anxiety or depression, it is important to understand this truth so that we stop making judgments about why someone may be dealing with anxiety and depression. It's probably not what you think. If you insist on judging, then please judge correctly.

You will discover there are different types of anxiety and different types of depression. Therefore, it is extremely important to know this if you or someone you love is faced with either or, God forbid, both. Just know that anxiety and depression are both equal opportunity destroyers, and they do not discriminate. I have listed below some statistics that you may not be aware of.

ANXIETY FACTS AND STATISTICS

*Note: These facts are taken from the Anxiety &
Depression Association of America website* (ADAA 2021):

We all experience anxiety from time to time. When anxiety and its symptoms begin to interfere with normal daily activities, is it classified as an anxiety disorder.

Anxiety disorders are the most common mental illness in the U.S., affecting forty million adults in the United States aged eighteen and older or 18.1 percent of the population every year.

People with an anxiety disorder are three to five times more likely to go to the doctor and six times more likely to be hospitalized for psychiatric disorders than those who do not suffer from anxiety disorders.

According to The Economic Burden of Anxiety Disorders, a study commissioned by the ADAA and based on data gathered by the association and published in the Journal of Clinical Psychiatry, anxiety disorders cost the U.S. more than forty-two billion a year, almost one-third of the $148 billion total mental health bills for the U.S.

More than $22.84 billion of those costs are associated with the repeated use of healthcare services as those with anxiety disorders seek relief for symptoms that mimic physical illnesses.

Anxiety disorders are highly treatable, yet only 36.9 percent of those suffering receive treatment.

It's not uncommon for someone with an anxiety disorder to also suffer from depression or vice versa. Nearly 50 percent of those diagnosed with depression are also diagnosed with an anxiety disorder.

Generalized Anxiety Disorder (GAD)

GAD affects 6.8 million adults or 3.1 percent of the U.S. population, yet only 43.2 percent are receiving treatment. Women are twice as likely to be affected as men. GAD often co-occurs with major depression.

Panic Disorder (PD)

PD affects six million adults or 2.7 percent of the U.S. population. Women are twice as likely to be affected as men.

Social Anxiety Disorder

SAD affects fifteen million adults or 6.8 percent of the U.S. population. SAD is equally common among men and women and typically begins around age thirteen. According to a 2007 ADAA survey, 36 percent of people with social anxiety disorder report experiencing symptoms for ten or more years before seeking help.

Specific Phobias

Specific phobias affect nineteen million adults or 8.7 percent of the U.S. population. Women are twice as likely to be affected as men. Symptoms typically begin in childhood; the average age of onset is seven years old.

Obsessive-Compulsive Disorder (OCD)

OCD affects 2.2 million adults or 1.0 percent of the U.S. population. OCD is equally common among men and women. The average age of onset is nineteen, with 25 percent of cases occurring by age fourteen. One-third of affected adults first experienced symptoms in childhood.

Posttraumatic Stress Disorder (PTSD) PTSD affects 7.7 million adults or 3.5 percent of the U.S. population.

OCD and PTSD are closely related to anxiety disorders, which some may experience both at the same time along with depression.

Women are more likely to be affected than men. Rape is the most likely trigger of PTSD: 65 percent of men and 45.9 percent of women who are raped will develop the disorder.

Childhood sexual abuse is a strong predictor of lifetime likelihood for developing PTSD.

Related Illnesses

Many people with an anxiety disorder also have a co-occurring disorder or physical illness which can make their symptoms worse and recovery more difficult. It's essential to be treated for both disorders.

Anxiety disorders also often co-occur with other disorders such as depression, eating disorders, and attention deficit hyperactivity disorder (ADHD).

Anxiety disorders are treatable, and the vast majority of people with an anxiety disorder can be helped with professional care.

DEPRESSION DEFINED

Depression, known as major depressive disorder or clinical depression, is a common and serious mood disorder. Those who suffer from depression experience persistent feelings of sadness and hopelessness and lose interest in activities they once enjoyed. To be diagnosed with depression, symptoms must be present for at least two weeks (American Psychiatric Association 2013).

The American Psychiatric Association's (2013) Diagnostic and Statistical Manual of Mental Disorders (DSM-5) outlines the following criterion to make a diagnosis of depression:

The individual must be experiencing five or more symptoms during the same two-week period and at least one of the symptoms should be either (1) depressed mood or (2) loss of interest or pleasure.

Depressed mood most of the day, nearly every day.

Markedly diminished interest or pleasure in all, or almost all, activities most of the day, nearly every day.

Significant weight loss when not dieting or weight gain or decrease or increase in appetite nearly every day.

A slowing down of thought and a reduction of physical movement (observable by others, not merely subjective feelings of restlessness or being slowed down).

Fatigue or loss of energy nearly every day.

Feelings of worthlessness or excessive or inappropriate guilt nearly every day. Diminished ability to think or concentrate, or indecisiveness, nearly every day.

Recurrent thoughts of death, recurrent suicidal ideation without a specific plan, or a suicide attempt, or a specific plan for committing suicide.

To receive a diagnosis of depression, these symptoms must cause the individual clinically significant distress or impairment in social, occupational, or other important areas of functioning. The symptoms must also not be a result of substance abuse or another medical condition.

Sure, we all feel sad at times, but normally these feelings pass within a few days or so. When there is a persistent sadness that begins to interfere with normal life activities, then it is time to seek help.

Many people with depression don't seek treatment for various reasons. My prayer is that with more education and awareness, more people will seek help.

DEPRESSION FACTS AND STATISTICS

According to the World Health Organization (WHO 2021), as of January 30, 2020, 264 million people around the world, and of all ages suffer from depression. WHO also predicted that depression would become the second most prevalent disease worldwide by the year 2020. We are there.

Depression is the number one cause of disability worldwide.

It's estimated that 15 percent of the adult population will experience depression at some point in their lifetime.

Approximately twelve million women in the United States experience clinical depression each year.

Nearly 50 percent of all people diagnosed with depression are also diagnosed with an anxiety disorder.

Sixty percent of people who commit suicide had major depression.

Seventy percent of prescriptions for anti-depressants are prescribed for women.

One in four women will experience severe depression at some point in life.

Depression affects twice as many women as men, regardless of racial and ethnic background or income.

In general, married women experience depression more than single women do, and depression is common among young mothers who stay at home full-time with small children.

Women who are victims of sexual and physical abuse are at much greater risk of anxiety and depression.

At least 90 percent of all cases of eating disorders occur in women, and there is a strong relationship between eating disorders and depression.

Depression can put women at risk of suicide. While more men than women die from suicide, women attempt suicide about twice as often as men do.

Only about one-fifth of all women who suffer from depression seek treatment.

Almost 75 percent of people with mental disorders remain untreated in developing countries with almost one million people taking their lives each year. Also, according to WHO (2021), one in thirteen people globally suffers from anxiety.

It is believed that these numbers are not accurate because so many are in hiding in shame, suffering in silence.

TYPES OF DEPRESSION

Major depression: Severe symptoms that interfere with your ability to work, sleep, study, eat, and enjoy life. An episode can occur only once in a person's lifetime, but more often, a person has several episodes. Depression affects people from every walk of life.

Persistent depressive disorder: Depressed mood that lasts for at least two years. A person diagnosed with persistent depressive disorder may have episodes of major depression along with periods of less severe symptoms, but symptoms must last for two years.

Note: Some forms of depression are slightly different, or they may develop under unique circumstances. They include:

Psychotic depression occurs when a person has severe depression plus some form of psychosis, such as having disturbing false beliefs or a break with reality (delusions) or hearing or seeing upsetting things that others cannot hear or see (hallucinations).

Postpartum depression is much more serious than the "baby blues" that many women experience after giving birth when hormonal and physical changes and the new responsibility of caring for a newborn can be overwhelming. It is estimated that 10 to 15 percent of women experience postpartum depression after giving birth.

Seasonal affective disorder (SAD) is characterized by the onset of depression during the winter months when there is less natural sunlight. The depression generally lifts during spring and summer.

Bipolar disorder, also called manic-depressive illness, is not as common as major depression or persistent depressive disorder. Bipolar disorder is characterized by cycling mood changes—from extreme highs (e.g., mania) to extreme lows (e.g., depression).

STATISTICS WITHIN THE BLACK COMMUNITY

"We certainly can't achieve our life's purpose when we are dealing with mental health challenges. Black people have so many issues just being black and dealing with society and racism. But many of us think we are good because we've gotten the education, the job, the house. In reality, it's not the case."

-Dr. Rheeda Walker, PhD

For a moment, I want to focus on some statistics in the black community that concerned me. As you read these statistics, I hope they are as alarming to you as they were to me. In my research, I ran across Dr. Walker's quote, and it is so powerful because it's true. Black people in the United States of America live under the constant and consistent stress of just being black. In today's climate of increased racial aggression toward us, it is no wonder the increase in anxiety and depression in our community.

Dr. Rheeda Walker, PhD, is a tenured professor of psychology at the University of Houston. She is a behavioral science researcher and licensed psychologist who has published more than fifty scientific papers on African American adult mental health, suicide risk, and resilience. Walker is recognized as a fellow in the American Psychological Association. She is the author of *The Unapologetic Guide to Black Mental Health: Navigate an Unequal System, Learn Tools for Emotional Wellness, and Get the Help You Deserve.*

BLACK AND WHITE

Sometimes, it really is black and white. In our respective communities, mental health is viewed differently. Communities of color have always had challenges when it comes to access to basic health care, and it's the same, if not worse, with mental health care. It's time we all take a circumspect look at these statistics and change our perspectives. Mental health issues are real and need to be addressed with knowledge, love, and compassion. Everyone yearns for acceptance, unconditional love, and support no matter what. Let's find it in our hearts to become that beacon of acceptance, unconditional love, and support—no matter what.

According to the Health and Human Services Office of Minority Health:

Black/African Americans are 20 percent more likely to experience serious mental health problems than the general population.

Adult Black/African Americans are more likely to have feelings of sadness, hopelessness, and worthlessness than adult whites.

Black/African American teenagers are more likely to attempt suicide than white teenagers (8.3 percent vs. 6.2 percent).

Black/African Americans of all ages are more likely to be victims of serious violent crime, making them more susceptible to post-traumatic stress disorder (PTSD).

Sixty-three percent of Black/African Americans believe that depression is a personal weakness, and only 31 percent of Black/African Americas believe that depression is a "health problem."

People experiencing homelessness are at a greater risk of developing a mental health condition. Black/African Americans make up 40 percent of the homeless population.

Black/African Americans, especially women, are more likely to experience and mention physical symptoms related to mental health problems.

Black/African American men are more likely to receive a misdiagnosis of schizophrenia when expressing symptoms related to mood disorders or post-traumatic stress disorder (PTSD).

Only about one-quarter of Black/African Americans seek mental health care, compared to 40 percent of whites.

Dr. Rheeda Walker's assertion that many black people do not trust "psychology" because scientists and psychology were used to "prove" that black people were inferior to white people is important to consider (Walker 2020). This alone is enough to understand why many black people will not seek help. If I think you don't have my best interest at heart, then I surely will not subjugate myself to your perverted view of me.

WHY IS THERE SO MUCH ANXIETY AND DEPRESSION?

"The reality is that we all know people who have had mental illness, depression, anxiety, and other problems. The more we talk about mental illness and bring it out of the shadows, the more understanding and compassion we'll have, and I think the better care people will get."

-Dr. Eric Achytes, Psychiatrist

As stated earlier, there is no single cause of anxiety or depression. In this book, I am particularly speaking to anxiety and depression in women. As research continues, there are some known causes and risk factors we should all be aware of.

Biological, life cycle, hormonal, and psychosocial factors that women experience may be linked to women's higher depression rate. Researchers have shown that hormones directly affect the brain chemistry that controls emotions and mood. Finally, many women face the additional stresses of work and home responsibilities, caring for children and aging parents, abuse, poverty, and relationship strains.

POSSIBLE CAUSES OF ANXIETY

hormonal imbalances associated with menstruation, premenstrual syndrome (PMS), pregnancy, miscarriage, the postpartum period, perimenopause, and menopause

low progesterone levels

vitamin and mineral deficiencies, especially Vitamin B-12 and Magnesium

hypoglycemia (low blood sugar)

physical, emotional, verbal, or sexual abuse

digestive issues, including leaky gut syndrome

thyroid disorders

caffeine sensitivity

low sodium levels

mercury toxicity (tooth fillings)

parasitic infections

heavy metal toxicity

exposure to toxins and poisons

certain food sensitivity (poor diet)

candida (yeast)

chronic inflammation

cardiac arrhythmia's

stress (high cortisol levels)

sleep deprivation

gluten sensitivity

low-grade infections

genetic disposition

emf (electromagnetic frequencies for fields) radiation exposure

side effects from medications

unresolved personal problems

life circumstances: personal, family, financial, relational, employment, career

POSSIBLE CAUSES OF DEPRESSION

hormonal imbalances associated with menstruation, Premenstrual syndrome (PMS), pregnancy, miscarriage, the postpartum period, perimenopause, and menopause

physical, emotional, verbal, or sexual abuse

alcohol and drug misuse

certain food sensitivity (poor diet)

brain structure

chemical imbalances of the neurotransmitters

difficult life-changing events: divorce, grief, and other losses

trauma

genetics (family history)

side effects from certain medications (read the medication insert carefully)

thyroid disorders

chronic Inflammation

toxicity from molds

vitamin and mineral deficiencies especially B-vitamins, folate, folic acid

emf (electromagnetic fields)/Radiation from medical procedures

coping with chronic illness, injury, or disability

the death of a loved one

medical illness, such as a stroke, heart attack, cancer, Lyme disease, and Parkinson's disease

stress, including stress at work and home, as well as stress brought on by single parenthood or caring for aging parents

life circumstances: personal, family, financial, relational, employment, career

Just as there are my possible causes of anxiety and depression, there are just as many if not more possible symptoms. You will find like I did, that many of the symptoms are almost the same.

POSSIBLE ANXIETY SYMPTOMS

No two people dealing with anxiety will experience the same symptoms. The severity, frequency, and duration of symptoms vary depending on the individual and his or her particular situation.

increased heart rate (racing heart)
irritability
nausea

dizziness

sweating (palms, forehead)

nervousness, restlessness

insomnia/oversleeping (hypersomnia)

digestive upset including constipation

crying

panic attacks

shakiness

hair pulling and twisting

rocking back and forth

chest pain and pressure (tightness)

heart palpitations

dry mouth

difficulty swallowing

nail-biting/inside of cheek biting

headaches/migraines

muscle aches and pains

night sweats

easily startled

fatigue/low energy

mood swings

feeling on edge

mind racing

difficulty remembering

shortness of breath

fear of losing control

excessive worry and fear

increased blood pressure

hot and/or cold flashes

sensitivity to noises

avoidance of anxiety-provoking situations

POSSIBLE DEPRESSION SYMPTOMS

Again, no two people dealing with depression will experience the same symptoms. The severity, frequency, and duration of symptoms vary depending on the individual and his or her particular situation.

According to the National Institute of Mental Health (NIMH 2021), symptoms of depression may include the following:

inability to concentrate, remember details, and make decisions

fatigue and low energy

feelings of guilt, worthlessness, and/or helplessness

feelings of hopelessness and/or pessimism

insomnia, early-morning wakefulness, or excessive sleeping (hypersomnia)

irritability, restlessness

loss of interest in activities or hobbies once pleasurable

overeating or loss of appetite

unexplained aches and pains

headaches/migraines

digestive problems

chest pain/irregular heartbeat

low libido

persistent sad, anxious, or "empty" feelings

thoughts of death, suicide, and possible suicide attempts

mood swings/rage

crying (possibly uncontrollably)

lack of motivation

withdrawing from family and friends

isolation

STIGMA ASSOCIATED WITH ANXIETY AND DEPRESSION

Stigma is a stereotype, or a negative view, associated with a certain person or group whose life experiences, characteristics, or behaviors are perceived as different from what is considered normal. Stigma is rooted in fear and ignorance due to misunderstanding and misinformation. Once stigma is internalized, it is often expressed in guilt, shame, and condemnation by the person experiencing the stigma.

The stigma of anxiety, depression, and all other mental challenges is the reason many people will not speak up or seek help. Part of the problem is that many people still believe that anxiety and depression are not real. Many people believe that the person only needs to try harder, have more faith, or they should simply get on with their lives. This is so dangerous.

Those living with anxiety, depression, or other mental health challenge tend to suffer in silence because they fear these harsh, insensitive, and flawed judgments. Fears are surrounding other possible repercussions are real. I experienced some of these fears as well.

Below are some legitimate fears people have around the stigma of anxiety, depression, or any other mental health challenge:

Limited career advancement opportunities due to a boss or coworker finding out

Employment discrimination due to a medical background check

Loss of certain social circles/friends/professional affiliations

Rejection of a spouse or even certain family members

Rejection and judgment from one's religious community

Possible custody battle challenges due to a parent using a mental health challenge as a weapon

Fear of health and life insurance limitations

*Note: I was personally denied insurance coverage twice because of "prescription drug use." Mind you, this was because of the medication doctors prescribed for me. These were not street drugs. Go figure.

In other words, there is a fear of unfair judgment and/or reprisal. I hope you now understand why someone may choose not to speak up because of the fear and shame of the stigma. Dr. Mike Friedman, a clinical psychologist, shares his views:

In 1999, the U.S. Surgeon General labeled stigma as perhaps the biggest barrier to mental health care; this stigma manifests particularly in a phenomenon known as social distancing, whereby people with mental issues are more isolated from others. Eradicating the stigma and social distancing of people with mental illness must be a top public health priority to improve worldwide mental health and reduce economic burden.

People with mental health issues tend to internalize stigma to develop a strong "self-stigma." This self-stigma will often undermine self-efficacy, resulting in a "why try" attitude that can worsen prospects of recovery. Further, as people begin to experience symptoms of their mental health conditions such as anxiety or depression, stigma may cause some people to try to avoid, separate from, or suppress these feelings, all of which have been linked to the worsening of well-being. (Friedman 2014)

CHAPTER 5 - LET THE CHURCH SAY AMEN

"Let me give you a new command: Love one
another. In the same way I loved you, love one
another. This is how everyone will recognize
that you are my disciples—when they see the
love you have for one another."

-John 13:34–35 Message Bible

Amen is one of the most common words you will hear during a church service on any given Sunday morning. At the close of a prayer, we say "Amen" to let the speaker know we agree with the prayer. We say "Amen" after a speaker's statement as a way of endorsing and cosigning in the affirmative. Amen is normally loud, strong, and bold.

Amen is a Hebrew word that means, I agree, so be it, or it is so. As you have been reading this book, I believe there have been many points I have made or will make where you can respond in the affirmative and say, "Amen."

As I now turn my attention to the church, I ask that you hear me out. You may not like what I say. But I sincerely hope and pray that you will open your heart and mind as I speak honestly and frankly. At the end of all my saying, please do me a favor and ask God to show you if what I am saying is true. If it is, simply say, "Amen."

As we agree, let's move past the *Amen* and work to rectifying the concerns I will address. I need the church, God's people, to come together collectively with a loud, strong, and bold "Amen." Are we willing to admit we have been blind and deaf to the cries of our brothers and sisters who are in pain? Those suffering from anxiety, depression, and/or any other mental or emotional challenge. Are you willing to challenge your thoughts and beliefs up until this point? Let me ask you another question. And please answer honestly. Would someone being challenged with anxiety and depression feel comfortable openly sharing that with you? What is your answer?

Amos 3:3 asks a question, *"Will two people walk together unless they have agreed to do so"* (CEB). We have to choose to agree to put down our views and thoughts and seek understanding for the sake of our brothers and sisters. We can only do that when we seek true understanding.

Apostle Paul addressed the church in Corinth as they were divisions among the leaders. I believe that we need to do the same concerning mental wellness. So I write his prayer here. It is my prayer.

"Now I urge you, brothers and sisters, by the name of our Lord Jesus Christ, that you all agree and that there be no divisions among you, but that you be made complete in the same mind and in the same judgment" (1 Cor. 1:10 NASB).

I have shared my story with you. I have been as transparent as I possibly could. I have bared my soul before you. I did so hoping to appeal to the humanity we all share. I intended to impart knowledge, strength, and courage to all who will read this book. What I wish is that I could have been this transparent and open while I was going through all of this.

My fear of knowing that many of my brothers and sisters in Christ would look upon me with criticism and judgment kept me bound for much longer than was needed. I've been a member of the Church for quite a while, and I know that any sign of mental or emotional challenges is met with ridicule, rejection, and rhetoric fueled by what I believe to be sincere ignorance. I'm not saying anyone is evil or being overtly malicious. What I am saying is that people just don't understand. Therefore, many people speak about things they know nothing about, and they speak injurious words. I, too, have been guilty.

In my first book, *Anger Unmasked: Facing the Truth*, I realized I made some ignorant statements about anxiety and depression. My remarks were not directed at anyone in particular, but they were not wise. For that, I sincerely apologize. I didn't know either. Well, now I know better.

All I'm asking is that we all take a step back and re-evaluate what we've been taught and how we have responded in the past to people struggling emotionally and mentally. Anxiety and depression are not new. Now they have a name attached to them.

"No test or temptation that comes your way is beyond the course of what others have had to face. All you need to remember is that God will never let you down; he'll never let you be pushed past your limits; he'll always be there to help you come through it" (1 Cor. 10:13 MSG)

This Scripture lets us know that our challenges are not unique to us. Every challenge we face has been and will be faced by others. The comfort is knowing that the Scripture assures us that God will never let us down, allow us to be pushed past our limit, and that He will always be there to help us come through it all.

Note: Contrary to what many teach, nowhere in this scripture does it say that God, Himself, caused the test or temptation. He's a good Father. What good Father inflicts his children with evil just to see how they will react? He is a good Father.

With all of that being said, I was *a statistic*. A born-again, spirit-filled believer experiencing anxiety and depression and not knowing that this particular struggle was common to man. Not just any man. But men of the *Bible*.

Up to this point, I don't remember hearing one sermon about believers suffering from anxiety and depression in a compassionate and understanding way. What I had heard preached is that there is no way a "true believer" could ever be depressed. I had heard it preached that to suffer from anxiety was a lack of faith and just proof that you are worrying and not trusting God.

As I told you before, one of the most common statements I was told is to pray and trust God. I am convinced that the people who told me that had no idea that many of their heroes in the Bible suffered from mental distress. If I were asked to grade the church and her response to those suffering from any mental or emotional change, she would receive *a big, fat "F."* It would be a failure because I still hear the same ignorance today.

My mission is to bring education and awareness to mental health. Why is it perfectly normal for us to have care and compassion for our brothers and sisters who suffer from diabetes, high blood pressure, and cancer but demonize people who suffer from any mental or emotional challenge? Why tell us to pray and trust God? Where is the same care and compassion? The first step on the way to understanding is to stop telling us to pray and trust God. Trust me, we are already doing that. Would you tell someone with cancer to just pray and trust God? No. So please stop saying that.

NO MORE TIME FOR IGNORANCE

Christians are not immune to or exempt from anxiety and depression any more than we are immune to or exempt from any other illness, disease, or disorder. We live in a fallen world, and we are susceptible to every problem this world offers.

Sure, we have the power of God and His Word, but as you know, it is never that simple. We all will have struggles attaining the promises of God at times, but we can, and we will. On the way, it would be nice to have some support from our brothers and sisters in Christ.

Just for the record, it matters not how much Bible knowledge you possess, how many scriptures you can quote, how many diverse tongues you can speak, how loud you pray, praise, or worship, or how much faith you have. My friend, *you are not exempt from life*! Life happens to all of us. As I've always heard, just keep on living. You have no idea what tomorrow holds.

It's time we stop making people feel like something is wrong with them when they face mental and emotional trials and tribulations. Didn't Jesus tell us we would have trial and tribulations? Did he limit it to any particular trials and tribulations?

We all experience dark moments in life. But praise God we know that He is with us no matter what we face. He promises in Isaiah 43:2 "When you go through deep waters, I will be with you. When you go through rivers of difficulty, you will not drown. When you walk through the fire of oppression, you will not be burned up; the flames will not consume you" (NLT).

What an awesome promise. I love that God says when you go "through" and when you "walk through," because that denotes that we will go through some difficult times in this life. We just have to keep going.

LIGHT IN THE DARKNESS

It's time we shed a light on the darkness so God's marvelous light can bring healing and deliverance. It's time for the people of God to understand that He can work through prayer, professional counseling, medication, supplementation, and more importantly, all of us choosing to understand.

Bishop Kenneth C. Ulmer (2020) made some powerful statements that say it all:

> "God is in the business of shedding light on the darkness. What we keep hidden as individuals or as a community can never be eradicated. It's by the grace of God that we have such resources, tools, and knowledge available to make sense of what was once confusing and bring healing to what was shattered. Mental illness isn't selective. Professional help, when combined with prayer, and with the comfort of a community of uplifting believers, is a gift from God."

THIS IS THE PROBLEM

A September 2013 Lifeway Research Study found that 48 percent of evangelicals, fundamentalists, and born-again Christians believe that with prayer and Bible study "alone," people can overcome mental illness (Scheller 2014). Really?

Would we tell someone with a brain tumor or any serious medical condition to just pray and come to Bible study? How silly would that be? Sure, they should pray and come to Bible study, but they also need to see an oncologist and other specialists.

See, it's this dangerous rhetoric and thinking that has caused so much hurt. I guarantee you that the same people in the survey go to the doctor themselves for the treatment of diabetes, heart disease, high blood pressure, and cancer. We are in need of a major paradigm shift in our thinking. God heals and performs miracles but let's stop limiting how He can do it.

We know that God performs miracles, and everyone prays for a miracle but that is not the norm. God never intended for us live by miracles. God can heal any way He chooses. So, how about we pray, read the Bible, and go and get some professional help just like you do for all of your ailments? We must be not only prayerful but practical. Faith without works is dead. We must be willing to do the practical things in the natural as we seek God in prayer to do the supernatural.

SISTERS LISTEN UP

It is quite a shame that we cannot be open and honest in the church. I talk to women in the church and especially those in ministry who will not admit that they are experiencing anxiety or depression. They will tell me their symptoms and describe everything they are going through.

As soon as I mention that it sounds like anxiety or depression, they push back and call it everything but. I try to reassure them that I know because I've been there and that I understand. Once they realize they can't fool me, then many will fess up. But there are still those who will continue running to the emergency room, hiding and trying to make it be something else. I understand all of that, but it will not help until they face the truth and deal with it.

I know women who refuse to go to a doctor and get on medication, but they instead "mooch" a Xanax from a friend when they find themselves struggling. Just so you know, that is illegal. Remember, I explained that medications can possibly be more harmful than helpful. So, I've warned these women who "share" their prescriptions that it will not go well for them if something happens to their friend. In this case, sharing is NOT caring. Why won't these women go to a doctor? You already know: shame and stigma.

SISTERS IN MINISTRY

Ladies, we are in a unique situation. We have the added pressure of ministry and all that entails. We deal with a segment of people in the Body of Christ who don't believe women should be ministers and pastors, so we have to contend with those folks and their opinions. We have to look the part, talk the part, and act the part. And we better not show too much emotion or show any vulnerability, or we are viewed as weak and unfit for ministry. Yes, all of that and more so, we carry this, and it gets tough at times. We look at other women and they appear to be handling it all in stride. Well, I've found it that many times it's just a façade.

As I have shared my story at conferences, in church, and on social media, I have had the privilege of talking with, praying with, and encouraging so many women who deal with these same issues. I have had people reach out to me that I have never actually met. I have women reach out to me because they cannot tell anyone in their own families or their churches what they are really going through. It is sad, but it is true. I am honored to share what I have learned to help others.

Sisters, we have to be the catalyst for change. Come out of the shadows. No more hiding. It's time to come out of this bondage. It's ok to admit that you are struggling, and you need help. We can help one another when we are open and honest.

> "My challenge to the church is that we might move beyond the whispering, the silence, the shame, and the stigma. Instead, let us understand and show how Jesus came seeking, saving, and He served the lost, and broken people around Him. We honor Christ when we join in His mission by doing the same." (Stetzer 2021)

Hosea 4:6 states, "My people are destroyed for lack of knowledge . . ." (KJV). Therefore, I am sounding the alarm and saying that ignorance is not bliss. It can destroy someone's life. We teach that the church is a hospital for the sick. Well, I've found that this hospital seems only willing to admit certain patients and only treat certain ailments. We cannot continue to ignore this very disturbing truth. Do we think that refusing to talk about emotional and mental challenges will simply make them go away? Nope, it just causes people to suffer in silence for fear of the stigma that we all know surrounds mental challenges, especially in the African American community and for us strong black sisters.

We are told that our ancestors lived through atrocities, so strength is in our DNA. We are told that we are strong, so we attempt to be strong. What does that mean? It's just pressure that we cannot bear up under. I think of the older generation who never talked about what they were going through. They were proud and kept all of the trauma, problems, concerns, and stuff all inside. This is not healthy.

Maybe that explains some of the high blood pressure, sickness, disease, and premature deaths? We were never designed to carry the weight of the world on our shoulders. I know...I broke under all of the weight. I refuse to even attempt to carry it anymore and neither should you.

BLACK SISTERS

Sisters we already have enough on our shoulders. From birth, we deal with racism, colorism, sexism, and it's just what we know. We exist in this world under pressures and stresses that are strictly unique to us. Our society devalues us, disrespects us, and demands more of us than our counterparts. We are maligned, and attempts are made to make us feel inferior because of our beautiful African traits. It causes many of us to try and assimilate and fit into the standard of beauty of the dominant culture. That pressure alone has been exhausting.

Well, I am pleased to see that many of us are beginning to reject all of that nonsense and embrace our unique beauty. I've always wondered that if my brown skin is so bad, then why do people burn in the sun to get a tan and then try to compare it to my skin? If my kinky hair is so unsightly, then why do people insist on admiring and touching it? If my big lips are so ugly, then why do people inject substances in their lips to plump them up? I'm just wondering . . .

To my beautiful black sisters, you are all beautiful, and you need to throw away society's warped view of who you are and walk in the elegance in which God created you. Hold your head up. Girl, come here, and let me straighten your crown.

AWKWARD MOMENTS

I attended a women's conference in the middle of the craziness I was experiencing. I was hesitant to go due to all of the weight loss. I was very self-conscious. As I was standing in line to enter the ballroom, a ministry acquaintance ran over, and we hugged one another. I had not seen her in a year or so. As we embraced, she whispered in my ear that I had lost enough weight and I didn't need to lose any more. It felt like a dagger in my heart.

As we broke our hug, I looked into her eyes and said, "I am not trying to lose weight." She stared back then dropped her eyes and apologized. She didn't say anything else, she didn't ask me any questions, she didn't offer any prayer. She offered nothing. We awkwardly stood there waiting to be seated in the conference room. We found our seats, and I sat in the session fighting back tears. I faked my way through the conference and went away sad.

Let me say, I was not and am not angry with my sister. She did not know, and I do not believe she was being malicious. It was just an awkward situation, and it just happened. In my case, it just added to everything else I was dealing with.

Please people watch your words. Remember your words have the power to heal or the power to harm. Proverbs 18:21 reminds us that death and life are in the power of our tongue (KJV). So let's choose to speak life to people and not death. And just food for thought, before you say anything to someone, ask yourself if God would say that to them. Then speak accordingly.

"Some people make cutting remarks, but the words of the wise bring healing" (Prov. 12:18 NLT).

"Gracious words are like a honeycomb, sweetness to the soul and health to the body" (Prov. 16:24 ESV).

WE ARE STRONGER TOGETHER

"Two people are better off than one, for they can help each other succeed. If one person falls, the other one can reach out and help. But someone who falls alone is in real trouble. Likewise, two people lying close together can keep each other warm. But how can one be warm alone? A person standing alone can be attacked and defeated, but two can stand back-to-back and conquer. Three are even better, for a triple-braided cord is not easily broken" (Eccl. 4:9–12 NLT).

Contrary to what people say, we do need one another. No man is meant to be an island. We are stronger together. Can you imagine how much better our lives would be if Ecclesiastes 4:9–12 was a reality in our relationships? We would be blessed, and we would be a blessing to many others.

Suffering in silence and isolation is a cruel existence. The loneliness, fear of rejection, and the fear of ridicule should never be the life of a Christian. Unfortunately, it is, and that is why I withdrew and suffered in silence for years. I have found that many are still doing the same thing. We must find a way to truly accept and love one another unconditionally. It's okay not to be okay, it's just not okay to stay that way.

God does not penalize, punish, or patronize us from our emotions, fears, anxieties, depression, or any negative reactions or responses—only people do that.

How is this possible in the church? What about unconditional love? What about bearing one another's burden? What about being our brother or sister's keeper? The church should be our safe place. Jesus ministered love and care for the hurting, the hopeless, the helpless, and He healed them. We are not Jesus, of course, but as His followers, we should emulate Him.

We need a seismic culture shift in the church. Look, we are all humans with frailties, weaknesses, and flaws. The Bible tells us to confess our faults to one another so that we may be healed. The Bible teaches that when one member suffers, all suffer. Oh, how I just wished we lived the Bible.

The Bible teaches us to confess our faults one to another so that we might be healed.

"Confess to one another therefore your faults (your slips, your false steps, your offenses, and your sins), and pray (also) for one another, that you may be healed *and* restored [to a spiritual tone of mind and heart]. The earnest (heartfelt, continued) prayer of a righteous man makes tremendous power available [dynamic in its working]." (James 5:16 AMPC).

It sounds to me that if the church would truly live out this Scripture, then we would have a healthy body of believers. It's time for the church to get healthy. A healthy church will produce healthy people.

CHRISTIAN COUNSELING/THERAPY

What about Christian counseling or therapy? There is an intense debate in the Christian community about the value of "professional" Christian counseling/therapy. Many people frown upon counseling using James 5:16 to argue their point. They claim that all we need is the Bible. I refuse to argue the issue. What I do know is that I have never seen James 5:16 at work in any church I have been a part of in more than thirty-five years.

I benefitted from Christian counseling/therapy. I know many others who have as well. Christian counseling uses God's Word to help an individual process her problems through the authority and power of Scripture. Counseling can be a powerful tool.

2 Timothy 3:16–17 states, "All scripture is inspired by God and is useful to teach us what is true and to make us realize what is wrong in our lives. It corrects us when we are wrong and teaches us to do what is right. God uses it to prepare and equip his people to do every good work" (NLT).

"Where *there is* no counsel, the people fall; But in the multitude of counselors *there is* safety" (Prov. 11:14 NKJV).

"If you listen to constructive criticism, you will be at home among the wise" (Prov. 15:31 NLT).

"Though good advice lies deep within the heart, a person with understanding will draw it out" (Prov. 20:5 NLT).

Therapy is a place where a person can share her deepest pain, fears, and cares with someone who will not judge her. A therapist is trained to help a person get to the root cause(s) of her problems and find ways to overcome them. It's just that simple.

Why is it acceptable to utilize other modalities or therapies like massage therapy, physical therapy, chemotherapy, etc., but not counseling which is talk therapy?

Isn't it just someone confessing their faults, slips, false steps, offenses, sins, hurts, pains, etc.? Isn't it James 5:16 in action?

THE IRONY OF IT ALL

When I think back over all that I went through, I am most disappointed and disturbed that I found no solace in the church. As a Christian, it is most disheartening when I remember the words and attitudes I faced when I found the courage to ask for help.

I was brushed off. I was told to keep it together. I was told so many dismissive things. My feelings were negated. I felt rejected by the people who told me they loved me and were praying for me. Their words did not match their actions.

I reached out to a sister who had an article on her website about overcoming depression. She told me that she would be glad to talk to me. We set up a time for me to call her. I called and she shared her experience. She then told me that I just needed to pray and ask God if I had any unforgiveness in my life. If so, then I needed to repent of it. Before I could even share what I was going through, she informed me that she had to go because she had just arrived to have lunch with a friend. She said she would call me soon and check on me. I am still waiting for that call.

Another sister told me she could tell something was wrong with me and she "figured" it was just something emotional. She never reached out to me or said a word until after the fact. I was angry at the time, but I now understand that people just don't get it. I tell myself that they just don't know what to say or do. I just don't want anyone else to ever go through this. We have to do better.

I am reminded of the words of Job when he was overwhelmed with so much loss and physical sickness. His so-called friends all had their opinions about why he was suffering. "Job responded, 'I have heard many things like these. You are all miserable comforters' (Job 16:1–2 CSB).

I appreciated the prayers but where were the empathy and compassion? I hate to even say this, but I received the most love and acceptance at a behavioral hospital. That is the saddest thing I have had to reconcile in my heart and mind. This should not be.

As I said, I understand the stigma, the struggle, the silence, the isolation, the lies, the fear, and the relentless stress of hiding. The devaluing effects of anxiety and depression, the devastation, the darkness, and the debilitating and pervasive loneliness. I know full well the angst—yeah—of not being understood in the church. I hope to change that.

"If one member suffers, all suffer together; if one member is honored, all rejoice together" (1 Cor. 12:26 ESV).

STRAIGHT OUTTA THE BIBLE

There is nothing new under the sun. Throughout the Bible, you will find the following words: downcast, miserable, brokenhearted, mourning, despairing, and some translations will even say "anxious" and "depression." As you know, some of our favorite Bible heroes faced some harrowing experiences from time to time. I love the fact that God allowed their vulnerable moments to be chronicled in the Bible. It should serve as a lesson to those in the church that we are all human and are prone to the same human experiences.

Another thing that we must understand is *there is no such thing as perfect faith.* There are what I call Faith Bullies in the church. I think they believe their job is to go around bragging about "their faith" and measuring everyone else's faith or lack of faith. No one has arrived and it's important to stop judging others because you, too, have weaknesses. Maybe yours are just not as obvious as others.

Let's take a look at a few of our Bible heroes and their struggles. God was faithful to help them even in their darkest times. He's the same God, and He will help us as well.

Elijah was afraid, discouraged, and weary.

Elijah was afraid and fled for his life. He went to Beersheba, a town in Judah, and he left his servant there. Then he went on alone into the wilderness, traveling all day. He sat down under a solitary broom tree and prayed that he might die. "I have had enough, Lord," he said. "Take my life, for I am no better than my ancestors who have already died." (1 Kings 19:3–4 NIV).

Jacob grieving over his favorite son, Joseph, whom he had been led to believe was dead.

"His family all tried to comfort him, but he refused to be comforted. 'I will go to my grave mourning for my son,' he would say, and then he would weep" (Gen. 37:35 NLT).

Moses and his constant burden of leading the children of Israel.

"Moses heard all the families standing in the doorways of their tents whining, and the Lord became extremely angry. Moses was also very aggravated. And Moses said to the Lord, "Why are you treating me, your servant, so harshly? Have mercy on me! What did I do to deserve the burden of all these people?

Did I give birth to them? Did I bring them into the world? Why did you tell me to carry them in my arms like a mother carries a nursing baby? How can I carry them to the land you swore to give their ancestors? Where am I supposed to get meat for all these people? They keep whining to me, saying, 'Give us meat to eat!' I can't carry all these people by myself! The load is far too heavy! If this is how you intend to treat me, just go ahead, and kill me. Do me a favor and spare me this misery" (Num. 11:10–15 NLT)

Job's tragic loss of his livestock, servants, children, devastation, non-supportive wife, and friends.

"Why wasn't I born dead? Why didn't I die as I came from the womb? Why was I laid on my mother's lap? Why did she nurse me at her breasts? Had I died at birth, I would now be at peace. I would be asleep and at rest. I would rest with the world's kings and prime ministers whose great buildings now lie in ruins. I would rest with princes, rich in gold, whose palaces were filled with silver. Why wasn't I buried like a stillborn child, like a baby who never lives to see the light? For in death the wicked cause no trouble, and the weary are at rest. Even captives are at ease in death, with no guards to curse them. Rich and poor are both there, and the slave is free from his master. Oh, why give light to those in misery, and life to those who are bitter? They long for death, and it won't come. They search for death more eagerly than for hidden treasure. They're filled with joy when they finally die and rejoice when they find the grave. Why is life given to those with no future, those God has surrounded with difficulties? I cannot eat for sighing; my groans pour out like water. What I always feared has happened to me. What I dreaded has come true. I have no peace, no quietness. I have no rest; only trouble comes." (Job 3:11–26 NLT).

"I am disgusted with my life. Let me complain freely. My bitter soul must complain" (Job 10:1 NLT).

Jeremiah, The Weeping Prophet suffered rejection, ridicule, loneliness, discouragement, defeat, insecurity.

"Yet I curse the day I was born. May no one celebrate the day of my birth. I curse the messenger who told my father, "Good news—you have a son!" Let him be destroyed like the cities of old that the Lord overthrew without mercy. Terrify him all day long with battle shouts, because he did not kill me at birth. Oh, that I had died in my mother's womb, that her body had been my grave! Why was I ever born? My entire life has been filled with trouble, sorrow, and shame" (Jer. 20:14–18 NLT).

King David was distraught, discouraged, sad, and depressed.

"The king was overcome with emotion. He went up to the room over the gateway and burst into tears. And as he went, he cried, 'O my son Absalom! My son, my son Absalom! If only I had died instead of you! O Absalom, my son, my son' (2 Sam. 18:33 NLT).

"Why am I discouraged? Why is my heart so sad? I will put my hope in God! I will praise him again—my Savior and my God! Now I am deeply discouraged, but I will remember you—even from distant Mount Hermon, the source of the Jordan, from the land of Mount Mizar. I hear the tumult of the raging seas as your waves and surging tides sweep over me. But each day the Lord pours his unfailing love upon me, and through each night I sing his songs, praying to God who gives me life. 'O God my rock,' I cry, 'Why have you forgotten me? Why must I wander around in grief, oppressed by my enemies?' Their taunts break my bones. They scoff, 'Where is this God of yours?' Why am I discouraged? Why is my heart so sad? I will put my hope in God! I will praise him again—my Savior and my God" (Ps. 42:5–11 NLT).

Jesus was in agony of the spirit. He said his soul was crushed with grief to the point of death. He was so distressed that He sweat blood.

The Bible states that Jesus was touched with the feelings of our infirmities. Isaiah 53 prophesied that Jesus would be a man of sorrows and acquainted with grief. (ESV)

They went to the olive grove called Gethsemane, and Jesus said, "Sit here while I go and pray." He took Peter, James, and John with him, and he became deeply troubled and distressed. He told them, "My soul is crushed with grief to the point of death. Stay here and keep watch with me." He went on a little farther and fell to the ground. He prayed that, if it were possible, the awful hour awaiting him might pass him by. "Abba, Father," he cried out, "everything is possible for you. Please take this cup of suffering away from me. Yet I want your will to be done, not mine" (Mark 14:32–36 NLT).

"He prayed more fervently, and he was in such agony of spirit that his sweat fell to the ground like great drops of blood." (Luke 22:44 NLT).

"Seeing then that we have a great high priest, that is passed into the heavens, Jesus the Son of God, let us hold fast our profession. For we have not a high priest which cannot be touched with the feeling of our infirmities; but was in all points tempted like as we are, yet without sin. Let us, therefore, come boldly unto the throne of grace, that we may obtain mercy, and find grace to help in time of need (Heb. 4:14–16 KJV).

As you can see, here are just a few of our Bible heroes who suffered greatly, and guess what? God honored them and delivered them. Even The Perfect One, Jesus Christ, suffered and God did not hold it against Him. That is why He is our High Priest. *He understands* what we go through. Praise God!

Let us show some understanding and compassion toward our fellow brothers and sisters. Instead of condemning one another, let's help each other up.

I'll say it again, "God does not penalize, punish, or patronize us for our emotions, fears, anxieties, depression, or any other negative reactions or responses. Only people do that." So let's commit to not do that any longer.

There is nothing new under the sun. *Let the church say Amen!*

Chapter 6 - Your Mental Health Matters

"What mental health needs is more sunlight,
more candor, more unashamed conversation."

-Glenn Close

"So now, may the God of peace make you His own completely and set you apart from the rest. May your spirit, soul, and body be preserved, kept intact and wholly free from the any sort of blame at the coming of our Lord Jesus the Anointed. For the God who calls you is faithful, and He can be trusted to make it so" (1 Thess. 5:23–24 VOICE).

"Beloved, I pray that all may go well with you and that you may be in good health, just as it is well with your soul" (3 John 1:2 NRSV).

Your mental health is important, and it matters. You are a three-part being. You are a spirit, you have a soul, and you live in a body. Your spirit, soul, and body are all interrelated, and whatever affects one, affects all. Your soul is made up of your mind, will, emotions, intellect, and your imagination. If there is an imbalance in your spirit, soul, or body there will be a manifestation of dysfunction. Where and how it shows up can vary from one person to another.

Therefore, you must begin to take your mental health seriously and develop a plan to protect your mental space. I will share with you later some ideas on how to do just that.

Unfortunately, what I've experienced and what I have discovered is that most people do not have a mental health plan. I didn't either. Where do we learn about the importance of mental health? Who teaches us the importance of spirit, soul, body harmony? We hear about mental illness but never about mental wellness and how to achieve and/or maintain it.

As we have discovered, there are millions of people all over the world who suffer in silence. I am on a mission to stomp out the stigma and judgment surrounding anxiety and depression and I pray that you will join me. *Let the church say Amen!*

We have also learned there is a myriad of causes of anxiety and depression. No two people are alike and neither will be their situation or their solution. We must address the spirit, soul, and body connection and deal with those issues with compassion and kindness. We all have issues of some kind, and we must have compassion for one another so we can all heal. We must holistically treat the whole person, or we will fail to achieve wholeness.

Go ahead and cry. It's all right.

". . . Weeping may endure for a night, but joy cometh in the morning" (Ps. 30:5 KJV). This is one of my favorite scriptures. It's very encouraging. I tell people that joy will come in the morning but it may not come tomorrow morning. So hang in there.

This part of the book was inspired by Wess Morgan's song, "Cry." I was driving down the road when this song came on the radio. This song was so powerful. I cried the rest of the way home.

Crying, weeping, and being able to allow tears to flow freely is a sign of a mentally and emotionally healthy individual. Crying is normal. A good cry is physically, emotionally, and psychologically cleansing as it allows one to detox negative emotions. It's effective at relieving stress, frustrations, grief, and sadness that we all face from time to time.

Dr. William Frey of the Ramsey Medical Center in Minneapolis discovered that emotional tears contain stress hormones and other toxins. Crying helps excrete these hormones and toxins from our bodies.

God knew life would be difficult at times and in His foreknowledge gave us tears by which to express ourselves and help us release and revive. Unfortunately, many people suppress feelings, emotional pain, grief, and stress, and it's proven to have devastating effects on the body. Elevated blood pressure, stomach distress, depression, and aggression are some of the issues that can arise from refusing to or suppressing the need to cry.

I was never a "crier." I did and would cry but not often and not long. What I didn't realize is that somewhere deep down inside of me, I subconsciously believed that crying was a sign of weakness. I was ok with crying but I felt it needed to be quick and you just move on. Somehow, I thought any constant crying meant something negative and would reflect on me as a "Woman of God" or "Christian." I never condemned anyone else for crying but I sure condemned myself.

As I shared with you earlier, my mother passed away on April 3, 2011. The chemotherapy and radiation devastated her body as the doctors treated the lung cancer. To watch her suffer and die like that was unbearable. Her death hit me like a ton of bricks. The pain in my heart and soul was indescribable.

For months, every time I closed my eyes, I would see her taking her last breath. It was so difficult. I tried to remember the happy times. I didn't know of anyone else who had dealt with this, so I just prayed and asked God to help me not see it. I dreamt of her often.

I cried a bit at first. Then, I was just numb. As time went by, I became very angry. Why did the doctors decide on the aggressive treatments when they knew how weak she was? I truly believed the doctors had experimented on my mother. You know we have a history of that happening in the United States when it comes to black people. Those thoughts were not healthy. I was not properly dealing with my mother's death.

I started telling myself the same thing everyone else was saying, "You know you will see your mother again. She wouldn't come back here if she could." "We as Christians have hope in the resurrection." Yes, yes, yes, I know all of that! I still can't shake these emotions.

I felt weak, embarrassed, and ashamed. I started beating myself up, "Marjorie, get it together. What's your problem? Why are you so weak?" I talked to people whom I thought would at least empathize and understand. Nope, they didn't.

I soon realized that I wasn't being honest about how I was feeling. I had been apologizing to God for my tears and my pain. I didn't want God to know how devastated I was. Silly me, huh?

I cried off and on uncontrollably at times trying to understand. The more I cried the more condemned I felt. I knew my mother was no longer suffering and was in a better place. I knew that I would see her again one day…yet I could not stop crying.

NOT AGAIN

Two years later, on April 21, 2013, my dad passed away. "Oh, Dear God, I cannot go through this again. Not so soon." I wasn't expecting his death. The doctors said he was fine. He would live for years. But later, we were told he had only weeks to live. I was not ready for this. I was a total wreck by this point. Again, everyone was reminding me how strong I was. So I kept trying to be strong.

As I was walking away from my daddy's casket crying, a pastor walked up to me and said, "why are you crying? Your dad looks so good!" That part! I tell you, I wanted to drop kick him right then and there. Who does that? How can someone say something like that? I was at my father's funeral, and once they closed that casket I would never see him on this Earth again. Are you serious? Come on, man! If you don't know what to say, please say nothing!

I was still reeling from my mother's death, and now my dad was gone. I was hurting. I was angry. I needed help. This is where my therapist, Dr. Thetford, came in. I was referred to a kind and loving Christian woman who shared the compassion of Christ with me. She helped me to understand that I was not grieving properly. I had suppressed the grief and was holding on to a wrong belief that crying was a sign of weakness. She reminded me that Jesus wept in the story of Lazarus (John 11 NLT). She reminded me that God gave me tears and that the ability to cry is a gift. "While Jesus was here on earth, he offered prayers and pleadings, with a loud cry and tears, to the one who could rescue him from death. And God heard his prayers because of his deep reverence for God" (Heb. 5:7 NLT).

She explained to me that I was trying to prove something—something that was not possible or even mine to prove. What I thought "being strong" looked like was undermining my healing process. I was allowing the words and expectations of others to cause me to feel weak and inadequate.

I told her how I kept being told, "Don't let this get you down, woman of God." Dr. Thetford responded, "Marjorie, these are your parents. You were a daughter before you were a woman of God." I sat there doing the puppy dog head turn. She was right.

The idea of being a *strong black woman* or any other type of strong woman is dangerous. We are taught this, and it is costing us in the area of our mental health. She is Jewish and said her culture has this same belief and it does not serve any of us well. We are all human, and our strength is in Christ alone. We need to learn to acknowledge that the only strength we have comes when we rely on God and not ourselves.

It's okay to be vulnerable and admit our pain, hurts, disappointments, and whatever else we are facing. It takes strength to be transparent. It's only human to be human.

CRY GIRL CRY

In one session, my therapist challenged my flawed thinking about crying. She challenged me to cry when it was obvious I was fighting back tears. She said, "Go ahead and cry —really cry and let all of this junk out." I was tired of crying and was determined not to cry. She told me I needed to cry, but I first had to give myself permission to cry.

She asked me what I was afraid of, then she answered and asked, "Are you afraid to let go and cry because you think you will lose control and not be able to stop? Are you afraid that someone in this building will hear you?" How did she know? I said yes, and before I knew it, the floodgates opened. I cried; this cry was one of the hardest, deepest cries I think I have ever cried in my life. For what seemed like forever, I cried and cried until I could cry no more. I sat there exhausted and feeling somewhat silly. Yet, it felt really good. She said, "Marjorie, you're allowed to cry whenever you feel like crying. Crying is healing."

My therapist was right. I needed to cry and release all of the pain. I realized there is a time to weep (Eccl. 3:4 ESV), and it was my time. Crying helped me begin to process the grief. I learned that crying is a sign of courage and strength. It can help bring healing, and it did.

Healing began to flow into my heart and soul, and I felt the freedom. The Bible says in Psalm 56:8, "You keep track of all my sorrows. You have collected all my tears in your bottle. You have recorded each one in your book" (NLT). Well, my friend, God must have a really big bottle because I cried a lot of tears. I have learned to cry when I need to cry, and I love the freedom I have found in my tears. I think I cried more in those three years than I had my entire life.

Friends, I pray that you will learn from my life story that it's entirely okay to cry. Crying is therapeutic. I want you to know that when you're faced with circumstances and life challenges that seem impossible, please know that your tears are amazing gifts from God. Crying does the mind and body good.

Cry. Let people cry. Encourage them to cry. Stop telling little boys to man up and stop crying. It's healthy for them to cry. I always hear women talking about these "hard men" who don't show emotion. I'm pretty sure they grew up being told to stop all that crying. Crying is a sign of strength. *Go ahead and cry! It's all right!*

> *"The sorrow which has no vent in tears may make other organs weep."*
>
> -Henry Maudsley, British Psychiatrist

CHAPTER 7 - A. R. I. S. E., FIGHT & WIN... IT'S YOUR TIME!

"For the Lord your God is going with you! He will fight for you against your enemies, and he will give you victory."

-Deuteronomy 20:4 NLT

ANXIETY AND DEPRESSION ARE YOUR ENEMIES

"He rescued me from my powerful enemies...They attacked me at a moment of distress, but the Lord supported me. He led me to a place of safety; He rescued me because He delights in me" (Ps. 18:17–19 NLT).

"The thief approaches *with malicious intent*, looking to steal, slaughter, and destroy; I came to give life with joy and abundance" (John 10:10 VOICE).

Anxiety and depression are evil no matter the root cause. They are powerful enemies. They are enemies of the cross, of Jesus Christ, and all that He died to provide us. Therefore, you must see them as evil twins, an unholy alliance sent from the pit of hell to steal your peace and joy. If left unchallenged, they will destroy your dreams, your relationships, your health, and possibly kill you.

Anxiety and depression are:

1. Deceptive because they can cause you to view God incorrectly.

2. Devaluing because they can cause you to view yourself through a distorted lens.

3. Devastating because they can cause you to feel emotionally and physically ravaged.

Struggling with the enemies of anxiety and depression for over three years was so debilitating. I knew I believed God and His Word, but the longer I stayed in the fight the more the deception started to creep in. Psalm 13 describes how I was "feeling" at my lowest point.

"O Lord, how long will you forget me? Forever? How long will you look the other way? How long must I struggle with anguish in my soul, with sorrow in my heart every day? How long will my enemy have the upper hand? Turn and answer me, O Lord my God! Restore the sparkle to my eyes, or I will die. Don't let my enemies gloat, saying, 'We have defeated him!' Don't let them rejoice at my downfall. But I trust in your unfailing love. I will rejoice because you have rescued me. I will sing to the Lord because he is good to me" (Ps. 13:1–6 NLT).

My faith was under attack. I was dealing with thieves who were slowly and strategically trying to destroy my life. I had to remind myself daily that God didn't do this to me. He is not a sadistic Father trying to teach me something as some would say.

Of course, God had not forgotten me, but the anguish of anxiety and depression was trying to convince me otherwise. There were times that I felt like anxiety and depression had the upper hand but I also knew that God was with me and promised to never leave or forsake me. I was so conflicted many days and ready to give up many times. But somehow, no matter how bad things were, I kept believing that I would somehow overcome all of this.

Anxiety and depression are thieves. When you hear the word thief what comes to mind? What does a thief do? A thief steals by taking something of value from its victim by stealth. Stealing everything of value in your life is the mission of anxiety and depression. They desire to steal your peace and joy. This is why it is imperative that you understand and stand up and fight the good fight of faith.

Jesus said in John 10:10 "The thief does not come except to steal, and to kill, and to destroy. I have come that they may have life, and that they may have *it* more abundantly" (John 10:10 NKJV).

"A final word: Be strong in the Lord and in his mighty power. Put on all of God's armor so that you will be able to stand firm against all strategies of the devil. For we are not fighting against flesh-and-blood enemies, but against evil rulers and authorities of the unseen world, against mighty powers in this dark world, and against evil spirits in the heavenly places. Therefore, put on every piece of God's armor so you will be able to resist the enemy in the time of evil. Then after the battle you will still be standing firm. Stand your ground, putting on the belt of truth and the body armor of God's righteousness. For shoes, put on the peace that comes from the Good News so that you will be fully prepared. In addition to all of these, hold up the shield of faith to stop the fiery arrows of the devil. Put on salvation as your helmet, and take the sword of the Spirit, which is the word of God. Pray in the Spirit at all times and on every occasion. Stay alert and be persistent in your prayers for all believers everywhere. And pray for me, too. Ask God to give me the right words so I can boldly explain God's mysterious plan that the Good News is for Jews and Gentiles alike. I am in chains now, still preaching this message as God's ambassador. So pray that I will keep on speaking boldly for him, as I should" (Eph. 6:10–20 NLT).

"I will exalt you, Lord, for you rescued me. You refused to let my enemies triumph over me. O Lord my God, I cried to you for help, and you restored my health" (Ps. 30:1–2 NLT).

If you are being challenged with anxiety and depression, please know that this is *not* the will of God for you. You have to know that you are in spiritual warfare. Your very life is at stake. It's time to fight back and win. Get angry and decide that you will not allow these enemies to overtake you.

IT IS TIME TO A.R.I.S.E.

"Arise from the depression and prostration in which circumstances have kept you—rise to a new life! Shine be radiant with the glory of the Lord, for your light has come, and the glory of the Lord has risen upon you" (Is. 60:1 AMPC).

A – Acknowledge your situation as a "fact" for right now. It does not mean you accept it as truth. Truth overrides facts. God's Word is Truth, and it will not fail—not one Word. Also, acknowledge you cannot fix yourself. You simply cannot. Ask God for help and direction and allow Him to order your steps. He will lead you along the pathway that is best for you.

R – Resolve and Refuse to stay where you are. Know that you can and will get through this. Resist the enemy. Reengage minute by minute if you have to. Do not retreat!

I – Involve others and don't isolate. This is a trick of the enemy. Get the medical help you need. God can use doctors, psychiatrists, medications, supplements, and whatever He chooses along with His Word to provide your way of escape. Talk to your family and friends and be honest with them about what you are going through. It's scary. I know. I pray that God will surround you with loving and kind people who will support you.

S – Stay in the process. Don't give in or give up. Set your mind to *win*. It will get tough at times. You will want to quit. But continue to fight the good fight of faith. Remember, there is no such thing as perfect faith. Just have faith in God and His love and care for you. It is perfect.

E – Expect victory and nothing less. Encourage yourself in the Lord. Enlist your faith friends who can encourage you when it's difficult to encourage yourself.

FIGHT

"The Lord says, 'I will guide you along the best pathway for your life. I will advise you and watch over you' (Ps. 32:8 NLT).

Yes, fight the good fight of faith. Trust God to lead you along the best pathway for your life. Your journey may look nothing like mine. You just have to remember that the storm you are experiencing will pass. The sun really will shine again.

SCRIPTURES TO HELP YOU FIGHT

"For the Word of God is alive and powerful. It is sharper than the sharpest two-edged sword, cutting between soul and spirit, between joint and marrow. It exposes our inner thoughts and desires. Nothing in all creation is hidden from God. Everything is naked and exposed before his eyes, and he is the one to whom we are accountable. So then, since we have a High Priest who has entered heaven, Jesus the Son of God, let us hold firmly to what we believe. This High Priest of ours understands our weaknesses, for he faced all of the same testings we do, yet he did not sin. So let us come boldly to the throne of our gracious God. There we will receive his mercy, and we will find grace to help us when we need it most" (Heb. 4:12–16 NLT).

"Do not be anxious *or* worried about anything, but in everything [every circumstance and situation] by prayer and petition with thanksgiving, continue to make your [specific] requests known to God. And the peace of God [that peace which reassures the heart, that peace] which transcends all understanding, [that peace which] stands guard over your hearts and your minds in Christ Jesus [is yours]. Finally, believers, whatever is true, whatever is honorable *and* worthy of respect, whatever is right *and* confirmed by God's word, whatever is pure *and* wholesome, whatever is lovely *and* brings peace, whatever is admirable *and* of good repute; if there is any excellence, if there is anything worthy of praise, think *continually* on these things [center your mind on them, and implant them in your heart]" (Phil. 4:6–8 AMP).

"He is despised and rejected by men, a man of sorrows, and acquainted with grief: And we hid, as it were, our faces from Him; He was despised, and we esteemed him not. Surely He hath borne our griefs and carried our sorrows: Yet we did esteem him stricken, smitten of God, and afflicted. But he was wounded for our transgressions, he was bruised for our iniquities: the chastisement for our peace was upon him, And by his stripes, we are healed" (Is. 53:3–5 KJV).

"Who his own self bare our sins in his own body on the tree, that we, being dead to sins, should live unto righteousness: by whose stripes ye were healed" (1 Pet. 2:24 KJV).

"And Jesus went about all the cities and villages, teaching in their synagogues, and preaching the gospel of the kingdom, and healing every sickness and every disease among the people" (Matt. 9:35 KJV).

"Are you tired? Worn out? Burned out on religion? Come to me. Get away with me and you'll recover your life. I'll show you how to take a real rest. Walk with me and work with me—watch how I do it. Learn the unforced rhythms of grace. I won't lay anything heavy or ill-fitting on you. Keep company with me and you'll learn to live freely and lightly." (Matt. 11:28–30 MSG).

"God heals the brokenhearted and bandages their wound" (Ps. 174:3 CSB).

"Behold, I will bring it health and cure, and I will cure them, and will reveal unto them the abundance of peace and truth" (Jer. 33:6 KJV).

"I sought the Lord, and he heard me, and delivered me from all my fears" (Ps. 34:4 KJV).

"When I am afraid, I put my trust in you" (Ps. 56:3 NIV).

"For God hath not given us the spirit of fear; but of power, and of love, and of a sound mind" (2 Tim. 1:7 KJV).

"For I am the Lord your God who takes hold of your right hand and who says to you, Do not fear, I will help you" (Is. 41:13 NASB).

"No weapon formed against you shall prosper, And every tongue *which* rises against you in judgment You shall condemn. This *is* the heritage of the servants of the Lord, And their righteousness *is* from Me,' says, the LORD" (Is. 54:17 NKJV).

"O Jacob, how can you say the Lord does not see your troubles? O Israel, how can you say God ignores your rights? Have you never heard? Have you never understood? The Lord is the everlasting God, the Creator of all the earth. He never grows weak or weary. No one can measure the depths of his understanding. He gives power to the weak and strength to the powerless. Even youths will become weak and tired, and young men will fall in exhaustion. But those who trust in the Lord will find new strength. They will soar high on wings like eagles. They will run and not grow weary. They will walk and not faint" (Is. 40:27–31 NLT).

"Let all that I am praise the Lord; may I never forget the good things he does for me. He forgives all my sins and heals all my diseases. He redeems me from death and crowns me with love and tender mercies. He fills my life with good things. My youth is renewed like the eagle's" (Ps. 103:25 NLT).

"Unless the Lord had helped me, I would soon have settled in the silence of the grave. I cried out, 'I am slipping!' but your unfailing love, O Lord, supported me. When doubts filled my mind, your comfort gave me renewed hope and cheer" (Ps. 94:17–19 NLT).

"I am worn out from sobbing. All night I flood my bed with weeping, drenching it with my tears. My vision is blurred by grief; my eyes are worn out because of all my enemies. Go away, all you who do evil, for the LORD has heard my weeping. The LORD has heard my plea; the LORD will answer my prayer. May all my enemies be disgraced and terrified. May they suddenly turn back in shame" (Ps. 6:6–10 NLT).

"You have turned my mourning into joyful dancing. You have taken away my clothes of mourning and clothed with joy, that I might sing praises to you and not be silent. O Lord my God, I will give you thanks forever" (Ps. 30:11–12 NLT).

"I love you, Lord; you are my strength. The Lord is my rock, my fortress, and my savior; my God is my rock, in whom I find protection. He is my shield, the power that saves me, and my place of safety. I called on the Lord, who is worthy of praise, and he saved me from my enemies. The ropes of death entangled me; floods of destruction swept over me. The grave wrapped its ropes around me; death laid a trap in my path. But in my distress I cried out to the Lord; yes, I prayed to my God for help. He heard me from his sanctuary; my cry to him reached his ears" (Ps. 18:1–6 NLT).

"You light a lamp for me. The LORD, my God, lights up my darkness. In your strength I can crush an army; with my God, I can scale any wall" (Ps. 18:28–29 NLT).

"Yet I am confident I will see the Lord's goodness while I am here in the land of the living" (Ps. 27:13 NLT).

"Why am I discouraged? Why is my heart so sad? I will put my God! I will praise him again—my Savior and my God" (Ps. 42:5–6 NLT).

"The righteous person faces many troubles, but the Lord comes to the rescue each time" (Ps. 34:19 NLT).

"But God is my helper. The Lord keeps me alive! May the evil plans of my enemies be turned against them. Do as you promised and put an end to them. I will sacrifice a voluntary offering to you; I will praise your name, O Lord, for it is good. For you have rescued me from my troubles and helped me to triumph over my enemies" (Ps. 54:4–7 NLT).

I hope that these scriptures will encourage you as they did me. There are so many more scriptures that I wrote down, read aloud, confessed, and listened to daily. Immerse yourself in God's Word. In the Word, you will gain strength and hope to continue to believe amid any trial you will face.

As you pray and seek God for your pathway to health and wholeness know that there are things you can do. Sure, God can miraculously heal you and that's always the prayer. However, in my experience, I have found that miracles are the exception and not the rule. So what can you do as you walk out your faith? Ask God to lead and guide you. In the meantime, I have listed some suggestions that you might find helpful.

God's Word is true no matter what happens. We just have to hold on to what we believe even when the circumstances are not lining up. God is faithful to His Word even when we are faithless (2 Tim. 2:13, ESV).

HOLISTIC APPROACH TO HEALTH AND WELLNESS

Your journey will be your journey. You may benefit from one or all of the different modalities. Remember, God will advise you and watch over you.

A Holistic health approach is based on the idea that well-being is a connection between mind, body, and spirit, and individuals are composed of all these parts. When one of these parts is off-balance, an individual's well-being can be affected: physical, biological, social, and spiritual. With this in mind, holistic health focuses on the healing and maintenance of the whole person, rather than just a single symptom.

A holistic health approach promotes a healthy diet of natural/whole foods and avoids processed and junk food products. It uses natural herbs, minerals, vitamins, and supplements to help achieve a healthy body and soul. It encourages healthy and meaningful relationships with yourself and others. It understands the importance of a healthy and productive spiritual life.

Complementary and alternative medicine aims to cure the human body of illness and disease through methods that do not include prescription drugs, invasive procedures, or other "traditional" medical practices. Acupuncturists, herbalists, chiropractors, aroma-therapists, naturopaths, reflexologists, and

148

other professionals all consider themselves to practice alternative medicine.

SELF-CARE IS THE BEST CARE

I say, "Self-care is the best care! Take care of yourself spiritually, physically, emotionally, etc. first. Then you will have the capacity to care for others."

On every flight, you're asked to secure your oxygen mask before helping others in the event of an inflight emergency. This is a powerful and practical truth we should consider for our daily lives. How many of us find ourselves out of "oxygen," so to speak. Yet, we are still trying to help others. This is not healthy or wise. We must take care of ourselves first. It may sound selfish, but it's quite the opposite. A healthy you can offer help and support to others.

SELF-CARE TIPS

I will list a few things I think could be helpful. I am not a physician or medical provider, so please consult your physician or medical provider before taking any supplement, vitamin, mineral, or therapy.

Prayer, reading the Bible, and spending quality time with God are all necessary. Talk to God and let Him talk to you. Praise and worship God no matter what. It may be tough at times but just tell Him. Thank Him as you know He's working it all out. Be honest with God. He already knows, so just be honest. Any good father wants what's best for his child. Would you be angry if your child came to you upset, hurt, and crying? Of course not.

Take time to receive Holy Communion to remember and celebrate the death of Jesus Christ. Isaiah 53:5 states, "But He was wounded for our transgressions, He was crushed for our wickedness [our sin, our injustice, our wrongdoing]; The punishment [required] for our well-being *fell* on Him, And by His stripes (wounds) we are healed" (AMP). Remind yourself daily of Christ's bodily sacrifice for your healing (1 Cor. 11 NLT).

Be nice to yourself. Be patient and give yourself grace. Take it one day at a time.

Surround yourself with positive and uplifting people. Avoid negative people who wish only to dump on you. You know the ones.

Learn to say *no*. You are *not* the savior of the world. One of the healthiest and most empowering things you can do is say no. If you can't do it or don't want to do it, then say no. No explanations are needed.

Talking out your problems with those who love and support you. Sometimes, you just need to talk and get it out. Find people who will listen and not judge you or try to solve your problems.

Journaling may be helpful as well. Sometimes, I write down my feelings and thoughts as a way to get them out of my head. I pray about it and ask God to help me process it.

Prioritize what is most important in your life. Determine if what you are doing is a God thing or just a good thing. Don't waste your time and energy on things that do not matter.

Seek professional help if you need it. It's perfectly okay to pray, go to the altar, and go see a therapist. Interview the therapist and determine if you feel comfortable. Keep searching until you find a therapist you feel comfortable with. If you need support, ask a friend to go to the appointment with you. They can sit in the lobby. Just knowing someone who loves you is there may be helpful.

Take up a hobby or try something new you've always thought of doing. Volunteer your time to help the not so fortunate. Go back to school or join a group of your interests. Read a book.

Go to a painting class or just go grab a canvas and some paint. There are so many creative things you can do.

Invite some people over and play games, watch a movie, or cookout your favorite foods. Sometimes you have to push yourself. You will be glad you did. Try your best not to isolate and withdraw from family and friends.

Go bowling, go to the movies, meet some friends for lunch or dinner. Play pool, go skating. Think of something fun and go do it. One of my favorite things is going to the beach. I always feel better at the beach.

Adopt a healthier diet. Yes, that part. Avoid sugar, table salt, white flour, dairy, caffeine, gluten, wheat (if you are sensitive). Eat foods God created in as close to its natural state. Eat plenty of veggies. Eat smaller meals.

Eat walnuts (2 ounces per day); they help the brain. Omega 3 and other healthy fats such as avocado, grass-fed butter, flaxseed oil, and extra-virgin oil also help brain health.

Eat lean proteins and try to avoid high-fat meats. Avoid highly processed meats as well. Proteins help keep blood sugar stable.

Drink clean water. Our bodies are about 60-70 percent water. So drink up. You need lots of water. Sometimes headaches, aches, and pain are just signs of dehydration.

Take probiotics and digestive enzymes to help with digestion. Probiotics help increase the good bacteria in the gut and crowd out the bad. Many of our foods are steeped in preservatives and our bodies struggle to break the food down. A digestive enzyme may be helpful.

Look into adaptogenic herbs like Rhodiola and Ashwagandha to help with balancing the body. L-Theanine is an amino acid that may help with anxiety.

You may need a multi-vitamin/mineral daily to ensure you are getting the proper nutrients. Be sure it includes Vitamin B complex and Vitamin D3.

Magnesium is a mineral that is responsible for over four hundred reactions in your body. Magnesium is considered "the chill" mineral. Most of us are deficient. It is available in capsules, gummies, and powder. CALM is one powder form that I use.

Research and consider essential oils like lavender, ylang-ylang, bergamot, chamomile, lemon balm, and clary sage to name a few. They may help you relax.

Incorporate teas into your day: chamomile, green, lemon balm, lavender, peppermint, passionflower, other herbal teas. Drink up they are relaxing.

Exercise is essential to your health. Walking is the easiest and cheapest way to get fit. Grab a friend and head out for a walk. Or put on your headphones and listen to some good music. Either way, move your body every day.

Add Epsom salt to a hot relaxing bath for about twenty minutes. You can also add in some lavender essential oil.

Practice deep breathing to get more oxygen in your body. It is relaxing.

Get out in the sunshine. The sun has healing properties, and it's one way to get your Vitamin D. It works wonders.

Build and maintain quality relationships. Having the right relationships are crucial to your well-being. Choose your relationships well. Avoid toxic and draining ones. Set boundaries with people and make them honor the boundaries you set.

Sleep is crucial. Got to bed. Turn off the TV. Put down the cell phone. Try to make your room as dark as possible and as cool as possible. You heal as you sleep.

Music is good for the soul. Turn up the volume on your favorite music. Sing along and dance if you must.

Relax. Get a relaxing massage. I love massages. I make the last appointment of the day so I can come home and go to bed.

Laugh and laugh often. Laughter does a body good. Watch a comedy. Hang out with your funny friends and just laugh. Laugh until your stomach hurts.

Please do not self-medicate with alcohol or other drugs. It will *not* help. It will only make matters worse. If you find yourself tempted to do so, *please* reach out for help.

These are just a few things you can consider. I encourage you to do your research and seek the assistance of a qualified medical professional before you take any supplement or incorporate any protocol into your life.

WIN…IT'S YOUR TIME!

> "You were born to win."
>
> -Zig Ziglar

"For I know the plans I have for you," says the Lord. "They are plans for good and not for disaster, to give you a future and a hope" (Jer. 29:11 NLT).

"What shall we say about such wonderful things as these? If God is for us, who can ever be against us? Since he did not spare even his own Son but gave him up for us all, won't he also give us everything else? Who dares accuse us whom God has chosen for his own? No one—for God himself has given us right standing with himself. Who then will condemn us? No one—for Christ Jesus died for us and was raised to life for us, and he is sitting in the place of honor at God's right hand, pleading for us. Can anything ever separate us from Christ's love? Does it mean he no longer loves us if we have trouble or calamity, or are persecuted, or hungry, or destitute, or in danger, or threatened with death? As the Scriptures say, "For your sake we are killed every day; we are being slaughtered like sheep." No, despite all these things, overwhelming victory is ours through Christ, who loved us. And I am convinced that nothing can ever separate us from God's love. Neither death nor life, neither angels nor demons, neither our fears for today nor our worries about tomorrow—not even the powers of hell can separate us from God's love. No power in the sky above or in the earth below—indeed, nothing in all creation will ever be able to separate us from the love of God that is revealed in Christ Jesus our Lord" (Rom. 8:31–39 NLT).

God has a plan for your life. I'm here to remind you that you are more than a conqueror. You are already a winner. You may have forgotten that for a second, but girl, I'm here to stir you up and say *you are a warrior*. God has equipped you for the battle and *He is on your side*. You cannot lose.

I am your greatest cheerleader. I know you can get through this because I did. I just wanted to offer you the support I wish I would have had when I was fighting the good fight of faith. It may get tough, and you might feel like throwing in the towel. Don't get into self-condemnation because of some "temporary" thoughts or feelings. Don't give up or give in! Don't lose hope Keep praying, praising, and pushing.

Real hope in Jesus may include prayer, faith, medication, self-care, supplements, and therapy—whatever you need to heal.

Finally, I challenge you to help someone else in need and give them hope for better days ahead.

HOW CAN YOU HELP SOMEONE IN NEED?

1. Pray and ask God how you might be of assistance to someone else.

2. Let the person know that you love them and are willing to help however you can.

3. Listen and don't try to fix anyone. You are not a trained professional.

4. It is appropriate to ask someone if they are having thoughts of harming themselves. If they are, please contact a family member or someone who can offer assistance. Do not leave them alone.

5. Ask them what they need or want instead of assuming you know what they need or want.

6. Offer support, understanding, compassion, patience, and encouragement.

7. Listen without minimizing what they say.

8. Be there. Sometimes just being there is enough.

9. Offer assistance in making appointments or accompanying them to appointments if they are overwhelmed.

10. Offer to bring a meal, wash dishes, watch the children, or whatever. In other words, do for them what you want someone to do for you. Put yourself in their shoes.

In conclusion, by sharing my journey in the pages of this book, I have endeavored to look beyond the surface and unearth the seedbed of anxiety and depression.

I let you know who I am and that I understand. In doing so, I have shared my thoughts on the stereotype of the strong black woman, which has kept many of us from getting the help we need while we often suffer silently under the influence of prescription medication to mask our daily plights. I have also discussed mental health matters and how the Christian Church can help or hurt people who are dealing with mental health issues. My goal is for you to A.R.I.S.E., FIGHT, and WIN!

It's your time! I ask God to help you look beneath the surface so that you will judge correctly. In other words, that you will get to the seedbed (the root causes) of anxiety and or depression in your life. He is the Almighty God, Jehovah-Rapha, our Healer. There is nothing too hard for Him. He is well-able to restore health to you and heal you of your wounds.

I pray that God will lead you to your healthy place and that your journey is a smooth one. Remember, you are God's child. He is a good Father, and He will take care of you. I love you and my prayer is that you will experience God and His victory in your life. I honor your courage, and I know great things are ahead for you. By Jesus' stripes, you are healed!

ABOUT THE AUTHOR

Marjorie A. Smith is a wife, mother, and grandmother. She is also a licensed and ordained minister. She serves as an executive pastor, teacher, author, mental health advocate, and conference speaker. As a Certified Health Specialist and Certified Mental Health First Aide, she educates and empowers individuals to make informed decisions for a healthy, happy, and balanced life. In Beneath the Surface: Unearthing the Seedbed of Anxiety and Depression, she shares her personal struggle with anxiety and depression and her journey to wholeness and freedom. Because she understands the shame, stigma, and self-condemnation that can accompany anxiety and depression, she offers a powerful message of hope and inspiration to help you discover your pathway to wholeness and freedom.

REFERENCES

Foreward

Newton, John. 1779. *Amazing Grace (How Sweet the Sound).* www.hymnary.org/text/amazing_grace_how_sweet_the_sound.

Chapter 2

Hitti, Miranda. 2009. "Metoclopramide (Reglan) Drugs Get 'Black Box' Warning." Medically Reviewed February 27, 2009. https://www.webmd.com/digestive-disorders/news/20090227/metoclopramide-drugs-get-black-box-warning.

Ogbru, Omudhome. 2019. "Benzodiazepines: Types, Side-effects, and Addiction." Medically Reviewed November 12, 2019. https://www.medicinenet.com/benzodiazepines_sleep-inducing-oral/article.htm#can_you_get_addicted_to_benzodiazepines.

Chapter 3

Ashton, Heather. 2001. "Benzodiazepines: How They Work and How to Withdraw" aka "The Ashton Manual." Revised August 2002. https://www.benzoinfo.com/ashtonmanual/.

Genentech. 2010. "Medication Guide: Klonopin." https://www.accessdata.fda.gov/drugsatfda_docs/label/2010/017533s046s048,020813s006s007medguide.pdf.

Hamzelou, Jessica. 2020. "Benzodiazepine Prescriptions Reach 'Disturbing' Levels in the US." Posted January 17, 2020. https://www.newscientist.com/article/2230379-benzodiazepine-prescriptions-reach-disturbing-levels-in-the-us/.

Johnson, Jon. 2020. "What Happens When You Stop Taking Benzodiazepines?" Medically Reviewed April 9, 2020. https://www.medicalnewstoday.com/articles/benzo-withdrawal.

Ling, Lisa. 2019. "This is Life with Lisa Ling: The Benzo Crisis." YouTube Video, 42:06, October 6, 2019, https://www.youtube.com/watch?v=zh_mTCzJ3j4&t=0s.

Ogbru (Gbemudu), Annette. 2021. "Benzodiazepines Drug Class: List, Uses, Side Effects, Types & Addition." Medically Reviewed April 1, 2021. https://www.rxlist.com/benzodiazepines/drug-class.htm.

Chapter 4

American Psychiatric Association. 2013. Diagnostic and Statistical Manual of Mental Disorders: DSM-5, Fifth edition. Arlington, VA. American Psychiatric Association.

Anxiety and Depression Association of America. 2021. "Facts & Statistics." https://adaa.org/about-adaa/press-room/facts-statistics.

Friedman, Michael. 2014. "The Stigma of Mental Illness is Making Us Sicker: Why mental illness should be a public health priority." Posted May 13, 2014. https://www.psychologytoday.com/us/blog/brick-brick/201405/the-stigma-mental-illness-is-making-us-sicker.

National Institute of Mental Health. 2021. "Depression." https://www.nimh.nih.gov/health/publications/depression.

Walker, Rheeda. 2020. The Unapologetic Guide to Black Mental Health: Navigate an Unequal System, Learn Tools for Emotional Wellness, and Get the Help You Deserve. Oakland: New Harbinger.

World Health Organization. 2021. "Mental Health." https://www.who.int/health-topics/mental-health#tab=tab_1.

Chapter 5

Scheller, Christine. 2014. "Hope for the Afflicted: The Church and Mental Illness." Posted July 21, 2014. https://

lifewayresearch.com/2014/07/21/hope-for-the-afflicted-the-church-and-mental-illness/.

Stetzer, Ed. 2021. "The Church and Mental Health: What Do the Numbers Tell Us?" Posted April 7, 2021. https://edstetzer.com/blog/the-church-and-mental-health-what-do-the-numbers-tell-us?

Ulmer, Kenneth. 2020. "Mental Illness is Hurting the Black Faith Communities. Prayer Shouldn't be Our Only Defense." Posted August 4, 2020. https://religionnews.com/2020//08/04/mental-illness-is-hurting-black-faith-communities-prayer-shouldn't-be-our-only-defense.

More References and Resources

Anxiety and Depression Association of America. 2021. www.adaa.org.

Anxiety Centre. 2021. "Anxiety Tests." https://www.anxietycentre.com/tests/.

Centers for Disease Control and Prevention (CDC). 2021. https://www.cdc.gov/mentalhealth/.

Depression Screening. 2021. www.depression-screening.org.

Hegner, Richard. 1999. "Dispelling the Myths and Stigma of Mental Illness: The Surgeon General's Report on Mental Health." December 13, 1999, https://pubmed.ncbi.nlm.nih.gov/11010620/.

Lifeway Research. 2014. "4 Ways Pastors Can Help with Mental Health." Posted September 13, 2017. https://lifewayresearch.com/2017/09/13/4-ways-pastors-can-help-mental-health/.

Mental Health America. 2021. www.mentalhealthamerica.net.

National Alliance on Mental Illness (NAMI). 2021. www.nami.org.

National Center for Biotechnology Information. 2021. "Depression Stigma, Race, and Treatment Seeking Behavior and Attitudes." https://www.ncbi.nlm.nih.gov/pmc/articles/PMC3026177/.

National Institutes of Health (NIH). 2021. "Depression." http://www.nimh.nih.gov/health/topics/depression/index.shtml.

National Mental Health Consumers' Self-Help Group Clearinghouse. 2021. www.mentalhealth.net/selfhelp/.

National Suicide Prevention Lifeline. 2021. 1-800-273-TALK (8255). https://suicidepreventionlifeline.org/.

Peer Support Space. 2021. www.peersupportspace.org.

Project Helping. 2021. The Stigma of Mental Health. https://projecthelping.org/stigma-of-depression/.

Psych Central. 2021. www.psychcentral.com.

Psychology Today. 2021. www.psychologytoday.com.

Ruggeri, Christine. 2018. "Learn to Recognize the 12 Signs of Depression." Posted May 15, 2018. www.dr.axe.com/signs-of-depression/.

U.S. Department of Health and Human Services Office of Minority Health. 2021. "Mental and Behavioral Health – African Americans." https://minorityhealth.hhs.gov.

WebMD. 2021. www.webmd.com.

CPSIA information can be obtained
at www.ICGtesting.com
Printed in the USA
LVHW051057281021
701787LV00010B/178